CCCC
CCCCONVIVIUMPRESS
CCCC

José Antonio Pagola

Following in the Footsteps of Jesus
Meditations on the Gospels for Year C

Translated by Valentine de Souza, S.J.

CONVIVIUMPRESS

SERIES MINISTERIA

2 0 1 2

Following in the Footsteps of Jesus
Meditations on the Gospels for Year C

© José Antonio Pagola

© Convivium Press 2012
All rights reserved
Todos los derechos reservados
For the English Edition

http://www.conviviumpress.com
sales@conviviumpress.com
convivium@conviviumpress.com

7661 NW 68th St, Suite 108,
Miami, Florida 33166. USA.
Phone: +1 (305) 8890489
Fax: +1 (305) 8875463

Edited by Rafael Luciani
Translated by Valentine de Souza, S.J.
Revised by Doris & Tom Strieter
Bible translation: New International Version
Designed by Eduardo Chumaceiro d'E
Series: *Ministeria*

ISBN: 978-1-934996-49-2

Printed in Colombia
Impreso en Colombia
D'VINNI, S.A.

Convivium Press
Miami, 2012

Following in the Footsteps of Jesus
Meditations on the Gospels for Year C

Contents

Foreword

Whoever gets close to Jesus has the feeling of meeting some-one strangely contemporary. There is something indefinable in his words and deeds that impact us even today, for they touch the core of our most vital problems and concerns. The passage of centuries has not dulled the power and life in them, especially if we are earnest and open our hearts to him with sincerity.

Not many men and women, however, get to know him. They haven't had the good fortune to listen to his message told in a simple and direct way. His teachings have reached them distorted by doctrines, formulas and abstruse theologi-cal debates.

Many ordinary, good people do not know the way to get close to this prophet, full of God, who welcomes prostitutes, warmly embraces children, weeps at the death of his friends, transmits hope, and calls everyone to be free to live a more dignified and happy life.

The appeal of the French writer, J. Onimus, should not come as a surprise: «*Why should you be the private property of preachers, highly qualified and learned men, you who taught such simple and direct truths, words that continue to give life to all people?*»

I have always thought that one of the best services I could offer is to place the person and message of Jesus within reach of ordinary people. This is the goal I have been pursuing for many years, as I comment on the Gospel text each Sunday in a simple manner and with more or less success. The convic-tion that motivates me is that faith in Jesus Christ is the great-est strength a human being can find to face life each day, the clearest light to live life successfully, the most indestructible hope to look to the future with confidence.

Many have distanced themselves from the church in these times because, perhaps, they have not found Jesus Christ in her. In a scene described in the Gospel of John, we are told that Jesus, seeing many people deserting him, asked his dis-ciples: «*You do not want to leave too, do you?*» And Peter, frank as always, replied: *«Lord, to whom shall we go? You have the words of eternal life. We believe in you»*. We too, for all one knows, may have to say the same thing: *«To whom shall we go?»*

JOSÉ ANTONIO PAGOLA

Part one

Advent

Stay Awake Always

« *"There will be signs in the sun, moon and stars. On the earth, nations will be in anguish and perplexity at the roaring and tossing of the sea. Men will faint from terror, apprehensive of what is coming on the world, for the heavenly bodies will be shaken. At that time they will see the Son of Man coming in a cloud with power and great glory. When these things begin to take place, stand up and lift up your heads, because your redemption is drawing near. Be always on the watch, and pray that you may be able to escape all that is about to happen, and that you may be able to stand before the Son of Man"* ».

Advent

25

The apocalyptic discourses found in the Gospels reflect the fears and uncertainty of those fragile and vulnerable first Christian communities surrounded by the vast Roman Empire. They are caught up in conflicts and persecutions, their future in the balance, uncertain when their beloved Lord Jesus would come again.

The warnings in these discourses also represent, in large part, those warnings that the Christians made to each other recalling Jesus' message to them. The call to keep awake, taking care to pray and to have faith, is a characteristic original feature of his Gospel and of his prayer.

So the words we hear today after many centuries are not directed to audiences other than us. These are appeals that we who belong to the church of Jesus must heed in the midst of the difficulties and uncertainties of these times.

The church today sometimes goes about like an old woman bent by the weight of centuries of strife and burdens of the past. With head bowed, aware of its errors and sins, she is unable to display with pride her former glory and power. It is time to listen to the appeal that Jesus makes to all of us.

«*Wake up*», encourage one another. «*Lift up your heads*» with confidence. Do not look at the future, stuck in your calculations and forewarnings. Your liberation is at hand. One day you will no longer be crushed, oppressed or tempted to discouragement. Jesus Christ is your liberator.

But there are ways of living life that prevent many from walking with their heads held up, trusting in the final liberation. Hence, Jesus is saying «Be careful, so that your mind is not fogged up». Do not become accustomed to living with a heart grown hard and callous, looking to fill your life with comfort and pleasure, indifferent to the heavenly Father and his children who suffer on earth. That kind of life will make you increasingly less humane, «Stay awake always». Awaken the faith of your communities and take care to listen to my gospel. Be more diligent about practicing my presence among yourselves. Don't let your communities remain fast asleep. Keep asking for strength. How can we «keep standing before the Son of Man»? How will we follow in the footsteps of Jesus unless the Father sustains us?

2

In the Setting of the Desert

PREPARE THE WAY FOR THE LORD

LUKE 3:1-6

SECOND SUNDAY OF SDVENT

«*In the fifteenth year of the reign of Tiberius Caesar —when Pontius Pilate was governor of Judea, Herod tetrarch of Galilee, his brother Philip tetrarch of Iturea and Traconitis, and Lysanias tetrarch of Abilene— during the high priesthood of Annas and Caiaphas, the word of God came to John son of Zechariah*

in the desert. He went into all the country around the Jordan,
preaching a baptism of repentance for the forgiveness of sins. As
is written in the book of the words of Isaiah the prophet: "A
voice of one calling in the desert, 'Prepare the way for the Lord,
make straight paths for him. Every valley shall be filled in, every
mountain and hill made low. The crooked roads shall become
straight, the rough ways smooth. And all mankind will see
God's salvation'"».

Luke is keen on reporting in detail the names of the persons who, at the time, controlled the different spheres of political and religious power. They plan and direct everything. Nevertheless, the decisive event of Jesus takes place outside the sphere of their influence and power without their becoming aware of or making decisions about anything.

That is the way what is essential in the world and in our lives always happens. It is how salvation and the grace of God enter human history. What is essential is not in the hands of those who hold power. Luke puts it tersely: *«The word of God came to John in the desert»*, not to Imperial Rome, nor to the sacred precincts of the temple in Jerusalem.

Nowhere else than in the desert can one hear the call of God to change the world. The desert is the realm of the truth, the place where one lives on essentials. There is no room for the superfluous. You cannot keep accumulating things that are not needed. Luxury and ostentation are inconceivable. It is crucial here to find the right way to live.

That is why some prophets longed so much for the desert, a symbol of a simpler life, better rooted in what matters, still undistorted by infidelity to God and by all the injustice done to people. In this setting of the desert, John proclaims the magnificent symbol of *«baptism»*, the defining moment of conversion, purification, pardon, and the beginning of a new life.

How are we responding today to this call? John again takes up an image from Isaiah: *«Prepare the way of the Lord»*. The paths in our lives are strewn with obstacles and resistance.

They make it difficult for God to reach our hearts and communities, our church and our world. God is always near. It is we who must open up paths to receive him who is incarnate in Jesus.

The images from the prophet Isaiah invite us to make basic, fundamental decisions:

- Secure the essentials undistracted by what is less important.
- Make right what we as a society have been deforming.
- Make straight our crooked ways.
- Face the reality of our lives to recover a readiness for conversion.
- Take great care of the baptism of our children.
- We need, in the first place, *a baptism of conversion.*

28

3

Share with Those Who Don't Have

«*"What should we do then?" the crowd asked. John answered, "The man with two tunics should share with him who has none, and the one who has food should do the same". Tax collectors also came to be baptized. "Teacher", they asked, "what should we do?" "Don't collect any more than you are required to", he told them. Then some soldiers asked him, "And what should we do?" He replied, "Don't extort money and don't accuse people falsely —be content with your pay".*

The people were waiting expectantly and were all wondering in their hearts if John might possibly be the Christ. John answered them all, "I baptize you with water. But one more powerful than I will come, the thongs of whose sandals I am not worthy to untie. He will baptize you with the Holy Spirit and with fire. His winnowing fork is in his hand to clear his thresh-

ing floor and to gather the wheat into his barn, but he will burn up the chaff with unquenchable fire". And with many other words John exhorted the people and preached the good news to them».

The message from John the Baptist in the desert touched the hearts of people. His call to conversion and to a life more faithful to God awakened in many a concrete concern: *what shall we do?* It is a question that always comes up when we hear a revolutionary call and are at a loss for an answer.

John does not suggest any religious rites, norms, or precepts. It is not a question of doing new things or assuming new responsibilities, but of living life differently, of making it more humane, of manifesting something that is already in our hearts: the desire for a life that is more just, dignified and fraternal.

What is crucial and realistic is to open our hearts to God, while becoming aware of the needs of those who suffer. John hits upon a concise answer in a formula that is awesome for its simplicity and truth: «*The man who has two tunics should share with him who has none, and the one who has food should do the same*». It is that simple and clear.

What do we have to say on hearing this message, we who live in a world where a third of humanity lives in misery, struggling for survival every day? Isn't it shameful to continue to pack our closets with all kinds of «*tunics*» and stuff our fridges full of food? How do we Christians respond to such a simple human appeal? Do we not have to open our minds and hearts to becoming more vividly aware of the kind of insensitivity and slavery that keeps us bound to an affluence that impedes our becoming more humane?

While we are rightly concerned with many current issues of our Christian faith aren't we aware that we live «trapped in a bourgeois religion»? The way we live our Christian faith doesn't seem to have the power to transform an affluent society. On the contrary, it is this society that is enervating the heart of the religion of Jesus. It drains our following of Christ of such authentic values as solidarity, defense of the poor, compassion and justice.

So, appreciate more and be grateful for the struggle of so many people rebelling against this «captivity». Get involved in concrete acts of solidarity with the poor, and foster a simpler, more austere and humane lifestyle.

4
Characteristics of Mary

BLESSED ARE YOU AMONG WOMEN

LUKE 1:39-45

FOURTH SUNDAY OF ADVENT

> «*At that time Mary got ready and hurried to a town in the hill country of Judea, where she entered Zechariah's home and greeted Elizabeth. When Elizabeth heard Mary's greeting, the baby leaped in her womb, and Elizabeth was filled with the Holy Spirit. In a loud voice she exclaimed: "Blessed are you among women, and blessed is the child you will bear! But why am I so favored, that the mother of my Lord should come to me? As soon as the sound of your greeting reached my ears, the baby in my womb leaped for joy. Blessed is she who has believed that what the Lord has said to her will be accomplished!"*».

Mary's visit to Elizabeth allows Luke the evangelist to connect John and Jesus even before their births. The scene is charged with a special atmosphere. The two are to be mothers. They have been called to collaborate in God's plan. No men are mentioned. Zacharias has been struck dumb and Joseph is surprisingly absent. The two women hold the stage.

Mary, who has hurriedly come from Nazareth, becomes the central figure. Everything revolves around her and her Son. Her person shines with features more authentic than many others that have been added in later years, due to advocacy and the conferring of titles far removed from the milieu of the Gospels.

Mary, «the mother of my Lord», Elizabeth proclaims with loud cries, filled with the Holy Spirit. The same confession is true for followers of Jesus. Mary is, above all, the Mother of our Lord. This is the point of departure for her greatness. The early Christians never separate Mary from Jesus. They are inseparable. «Blessed by God among all women», she gives us Jesus: blessed is the fruit of her womb.

Mary is the one who believed. Elizabeth declares her blessed because *«she believed»*. Mary is great, not just for her biological motherhood, but for having heard with faith the call of God to be the Mother of the Savior. She knew how to listen to God. She kept his word in her heart; she has pondered it; faithful to her calling, she has put it into practice. Mary is a woman of faith.

Mary, the evangelizer, offers to everyone God's salvation that she has received in her own Son. This is the greatness of her mission and service. According to the story, Mary evangelizes not only with her words and gestures, but also because wherever she goes, she takes with her the person of Jesus and his Spirit. It is, in essence, the act of an evangelizer.

Mary is the bearer of joy. The greeting of Mary spreads the joy that comes from her Son Jesus. She has been the first to hear God's invitation: *«Rejoice . . . the Lord is with thee»*. Now, moved by an attitude of service and help to those who need it, Mary radiates the Good News of Jesus Christ, whom she always bears with her. She is the best model of a joyful evangelism for the church.

Part two

Christmas Season

The Nostalgia of Christmas

A LIST SHINING IN THE DARKNESS

JOHN 1:1-18

CHRISTMAS DAY

«*In the beginning was the Word, and the Word was with God, and the Word was God. He was with God in the beginning. Through him all things were made; without him nothing was made that has been made. In him was life, and that life was the light of men. The light shines in the darkness, but the darkness has not understood it.*

There came a man who was sent from God; his name was John. He came as a witness to testify concerning that light, so that through him all men might believe.

He himself was not the light; he came only as a witness to the light. The true light that gives light to every man was coming into the world.

He was in the world, and though the world was made through him, the world did not recognize him. He came to that which was his own, but his own did not receive him. Yet to all who received him, to those who believed in his name, he gave the right to become children of God —children born not of natural descent, nor of human decision or a husband's will, but born of God.

The Word became flesh and made his dwelling among us. We have seen his glory, the glory of the One and Only, who came from the Father, full of grace and truth.

John testifies concerning him. He cries out, saying, "This was he of whom I said, 'He who comes after me has surpassed me because he was before me'". From the fullness of his grace we have all received one blessing after another. For the law was given through Moses; grace and truth came through Jesus Christ.

No one has ever seen God, but God the One and Only, who is at the Father's side, has made him known».

Christmas is a feast full of nostalgia. We sing of peace, but don't know how to find it. We wish each other happiness, but it seems more and more difficult to be happy. We buy each other gifts, but what we need is tenderness and affection. We sing to a child who is God, but the faith in our hearts has died out. Life is not what we want it to be, but we can't make it better.

Nostalgia is not only a feeling we have at Christmas; our whole life is infused with it. Nothing entirely meets our desires. No wealth can ensure total peace. No love can respond fully to our deepest longings. No profession can totally satisfy our aspirations. It is not possible to be loved by all.

Nostalgia can have positive benefits. It allows us to discover that our desires go beyond what we can today possess or enjoy. It helps us to keep the horizon of our existence open to something greater and more fulfilling than all that we know. At the same time it teaches us not to ask of life what it cannot give, not to seek from relationships what they cannot deliver. Nostalgia does not allow us to live chained down to this world alone.

It is easy to spend one's life suppressing the longing for the infinite that is alive in our being. We live enclosed in a protective shell that makes us insensitive to everything except what we see and touch. The Feast of Christmas, when celebrated in a spirit of nostalgia, creates a different atmosphere: at this time we grasp better the need for home and security. If we are in touch with our deepest feelings, we sense that God is our ultimate destiny.

Faith invites the believer to discover this mystery during these days, not in a strange, faraway land, but in a newborn child. It couldn't be more simple and yet amazing. We must come close to God the way we come close to a child: gently and noiselessly; no solemn talk, only plain words coming from the heart. We find God when we offer him the best we have in us.

Despite the frivolous and superficial atmosphere we create in our society, Christmas can bring us close to God, provided, at least, we live it with a simple faith and a pure heart.

2
Which Family?

«Every year his parents went to Jerusalem for the Feast of the Passover. When he was twelve years old, they went up to the Feast, according to the custom. After the Feast was over, while his parents were returning home, the boy Jesus stayed behind in Jerusalem, but they were unaware of it. Thinking he was in their company, they traveled on for a day. Then they began looking for him among their relatives and friends. When they did not find him, they went back to Jerusalem to look for him.

After three days they found him in the temple courts, sitting among the teachers, listening to them and asking them questions. Everyone who heard him was amazed at his understanding and his answers.

When his parents saw him, they were astonished. His mother said to him, "Son, why have you treated us like this? Your father and I have been anxiously searching for you". "Why were you searching for me?" he asked. "Didn't you know I had to be in my Father's house?" But they did not understand what he was saying to them. Then he went down to Nazareth with them and was obedient to them. But his mother treasured all these things in her heart. And Jesus grew in wisdom and stature, and in favor with God and men».

Today is the day of the Christian Family, a newly established feast to help Christian families understand, celebrate, deepen and live the spirit of Christ. It is not enough to defend only in theory the value of the family. Nor is it realistic to imagine the Holy Family in Nazareth as our model of the ideal traditional family. Following Jesus may at times demand that we question and transform models and habits that are deeply rooted in us.

For Jesus, the family isn't something absolute or set in stone. Still more, it is not the nuclear human family that matters. Instead, it is the great human family that we must keep building in order to fulfill the desire of the only Father of us all. Jesus' own parents will have to learn this lesson by undergoing misunderstandings and conflicts.

According to Luke, his heartbroken parents look for him after discovering he has left them without bothering to inform them. How could he behave in this way?

His mother reproaches him when they find him: «*My son, why have you treated us like this? Your father and I have been anxiously searching for you*».

Jesus surprises them with an unexpected answer: «*Why were you searching for me? Didn't you know I had to be in my Father's house?*»

His parents «*did not understand what he was saying to them*».

Only by delving into the profound meaning of his words and his behavior toward his family, will we discover that his prime concern is the human family: a more fraternal, just, and inclusive society, the way God wants it.

We cannot celebrate today's feast as responsible Christians without heeding the challenges of our faith. What are our families like? Are they committed to a better and more humane society or are they confined exclusively to their own affairs? Do they inculcate solidarity, compassion, a search for peace, and sensitivity to those in need? Or do they encourage an insatiable greed for prosperity and maximum profit, caring little for everyone else?

What's happening in our homes and families? Do we nourish our faith, remember Jesus Christ, and learn to pray? Or is it only indifference, unbelief, and emptiness that we see when it comes to dealing with God? Do we encourage a superficial lifestyle without goals, ideals, values or ultimate meaning to life?

Or are they educated to develop a healthy and responsible moral conscience consistent with their faith?

3

Follow the Star

WE HAVE SEEN HIS STAR RISE

MATTEW 2:1-12

FEAST OF THE EPIPHANY

«*After Jesus was born in Bethlehem in Judea, during the time of King Herod, Magi from the east came to Jerusalem and asked, "Where is the one who has been born king of the Jews? We saw his star in the east and have come to worship him".*

When King Herod heard this he was disturbed, and all Jerusalem with him. When he had called together all the people's chief priests and teachers of the law, he asked them where the Christ was to be born. "In Bethlehem in Judea", they replied, "for this is what the prophet has written: 'But you, Bethlehem, in the land of Judah, are by no means least among the rulers of Judah; for out of you will come a ruler who will be the shepherd of my people Israel'".

Then Herod called the Magi secretly and found out from them the exact time the star had appeared. He sent them to Bethlehem and said, "Go and make a careful search for the child. As soon as you find him, report to me, so that I too may go and worship him".

After they had heard the king, they went on their way, and the star they had seen in the east went ahead of them until it stopped over the place where the child was.

When they saw the star, they were overjoyed.

On coming to the house, they saw the child with his mother Mary, and they bowed down and worshiped him. Then they opened their treasures and presented him with gifts of gold and of incense and of myrrh. And having been warned in a dream not to go back to Herod, they returned to their country by another route».

We have grown too accustomed to hearing this story. Today, however, no one has the time to stop and contemplate the stars. It is not only a matter of time. We belong to an age when it is easier to see the darkness of the night than the bright spots that shine in the midst of any darkness.

It is still touching to remember that old Christian writer who, while developing the midrashic story of the Magi, imagined them following the small light of a star in the middle of the night. The narrative evokes the profound conviction of the first believers after the resurrection. The words of Isaiah were fulfilled in Jesus: «*The people walking in darkness have seen a great light. On those living in the land of the shadow of death a light has dawned*».

It would be naïve not to think that we are living in especially dark, tragic, and distressing times. However, is not this very darkness, frustration, and helplessness, which we are experiencing at this time, one of the features that almost always accompanies human beings on their journey over the earth?

In response to that question, it is enough to open the pages of history. Undoubtedly, we find times of light in which great achievements are celebrated, great freedoms sought, new worlds glimpsed, and new horizons opened for a more humane world. What happens next? Revolutions that create new forms of slavery, achievements that bring new problems, ideals leading to half-baked solutions, and noble struggles ending in mediocre compromises. It becomes darkness all over again.

It is not surprising, we are told, that to be a human being is often a frustrating experience. But that is not the whole truth. Despite all the failures and frustrations, human beings do recover, find hope again, and begin to move toward something indeterminate. Time and again, something within the human being summons him or her to life and hope once more. A new star always begins to shine again.

For believers that star unfailingly leads to Christ. Christians do not believe in any kind of new Messianism. So they are not prone to any disappointment. The world is not «a desperate case». It is not in complete darkness. The world is not only evil *and thus needs to change;* the world is reconciled to God *and can change.* One day, God will be the end of exile and darkness, and there will be total light. Today, however, we see him only in a humble star leading us to Bethlehem.

4
Reclaiming Jesus

THE LIGHT SHINES IN THE DARKNESS
JOHN 1:1-18
SECOND SUNDAY AFTER CHRISTMAS

«*In the beginning was the Word, and the Word was with God, and the Word was God. He was with God in the beginning. Through him all things were made; without him nothing was made that has been made. In him was life, and that life was the light of men. The light shines in the darkness, but the darkness has not understood it.*

There came a man who was sent from God; his name was John. He came as a witness to testify concerning that light, so that through him all men might believe. He himself was not the light; he came only as a witness to the light. The true light that gives light to every man was coming into the world.

He was in the world, and though the world was made through him, the world did not recognize him. He came to that which was his own, but his own did not receive him. Yet to all who received him, to those who believed in his name, he gave the right to become children of God —children born not of natural descent, nor of human decision or a husband's will, but born of God.

The Word became flesh and made his dwelling among us. We have seen his glory, the glory of the One and Only, who came from the Father, full of grace and truth.

John testifies concerning him. He cries out, saying, "This was he of whom I said, 'He who comes after me has surpassed me because he was before me'".

From the fullness of his grace we have all received one blessing after another. For the law was given through Moses; grace and truth came through Jesus Christ. No one has ever seen God, but God the One and Only, who is at the Father's side, has made him known».

All of us believers have multiple and very different images of God. From childhood we keep creating our own idea of him. We are conditioned by what we hear from catechists and preachers, what is transmitted to us at home and at school, or what we experience in religious celebrations and events.

All these images of God, which we form for ourselves, are imperfect and defective, and we need to purify them frequently throughout our lives. We must never forget this. The Gospel of John reminds us of a conviction we cannot escape that runs through the whole of biblical tradition: «*No one has ever seen God*».

We theologians speak a lot about God, always almost too much. It seems we know everything about him, but in reality no theologian has ever seen God. The same thing applies to preachers and spiritual directors. They speak with almost absolute certainty as if they harbored no doubts at all in their minds. In truth, none of them has seen God.

How then can we purify our images of God so that we do not distort the sacred mystery of his being? The same Gospel of John reminds us of the belief that sustains the whole of Christian faith in God. It is Jesus alone, the only begotten Son of God, *«who has made him known»*. Nowhere has God revealed his heart, or shown his face to us, as he has done in Jesus.

God has told us what he is like by becoming incarnate in Jesus. He has not revealed himself in doctrines or sublime theological formulas but in the awe-inspiring life of Jesus, in his behavior and message, in his commitment unto death, and in his resurrection. In order to draw near to God, we must draw near to the man in whom he comes to meet us.

Whenever Christianity ignores Jesus or forgets him, it runs the risk of distancing itself from the true God. It then begins substituting for him distorted images that disfigure his face. These images prevent us from cooperating with his plan to build a more liberated, just and fraternal new world. It becomes urgent to reclaim the humanity of Jesus.

It is not enough to confess a theoretical or doctrinal faith in Jesus Christ. We all need to know him through coming closer to him in a concrete, vital way, as is shown to us in the Gospels. In so doing, we learn to respond ardently to his plan, allow ourselves to be filled with his Spirit, enter into his relationship to the Father, and follow him closely day after day. This is the task a community must pursue passionately as it goes about purifying its faith. Whoever knows and follows Jesus will continue to enjoy in increasing measure the unfathomable goodness of God.

5

A New Spirituality

HE WILL BAPTIZE YOU WITH THE HOLY SPIRIT

LUKE 3:15-16, 21, 22

BAPTISM OF THE LORD

> «*The people were waiting expectantly and were all wondering in their hearts if John might possibly be the Christ. John answered them all, "I baptize you with water. But one more powerful than I will come, the thongs of whose sandals I am not worthy to untie. He will baptize you with the Holy Spirit and with fire".*
>
> *When all the people were being baptized, Jesus was baptized too. And as he was praying, heaven was opened and the Holy Spirit descended on him in bodily form like a dove. And a voice came from heaven: "You are my Son, whom I love; with you I am well pleased"*».

«Spirituality» is an unfortunate word. For many it can only mean something useless, detached from real life. What is it good for? What matters is what is concrete and practical; the material, not the spiritual.

However, the «spirit» of a person is something valued in modern society because it indicates what is deepest and finest in people's lives: the passion animating them, what inspires them and spreads to others, what ultimately they manifest in the world.

It is this spirit that encourages our plans and commitments and sets the horizon of our values and our hope. Our spirituality will reflect our spirit, our religion and our entire life.

The texts left to us by the first Christians show them living their faith in Jesus Christ as a strong «spiritual movement». They experience themselves as inhabited by the Spirit of Jesus. Only those who have been baptized with the Spirit are Christians. «*Whoever does not have the Spirit of Christ does not belong to him»*. Animated by the Spirit, they experience life in a totally new way.

The first thing that will change radically is their experience of God. They no longer live with *«the spirit of slaves»*, overwhelmed by a fear of God, but with the *«spirit of children»* who know they are loved unconditionally and without limit by a Father. The Spirit of Jesus makes them cry from the depths of their hearts, *«Abba, Father»!* This experience is what defines everyone in communities that belong to Jesus.

The way they live their religion also changes. They no longer feel like prisoners of the law, of rules and precepts, but are freed by love. Now they know what it is to live with a *«new spirit»*. They listen to the call of love and do not live by the *«old letter of the law»*, busily fulfilling religious duties. This is the climate we all should cultivate and promote in Christian communities if we wish to live like Jesus.

These communities also discover the true meaning of the worship of God. What pleases the Father is not rituals devoid of love, but a life *«in spirit and truth»*. A life lived with the spirit of Jesus and the truth of his gospel is, for Christians, authentic *«spiritual worship»*.

We must never forget what Paul of Tarsus used to say to his communities: *«Do not extinguish the Spirit»*. A church with the Spirit extinguished, empty of the Spirit of Christ, cannot live or communicate its true newness. It can neither savor nor spread the Good News. To develop a Christian spirituality is to revive our religion.

Part three

Lent

1

Recognize the Temptations

Lent

49

«*Jesus, full of the Holy Spirit, returned from the Jordan and was led by the Spirit in the desert, where for forty days he was tempted by the devil. He ate nothing during those days, and at the end of them he was hungry. The devil said to him, "If you are the Son of God, tell this stone to become bread". Jesus answered, "It is written: 'Man does not live on bread alone'".*

The devil led him up to a high place and showed him in an instant all the kingdoms of the world. And he said to him, "I will give you all their authority and splendor, for it has been given to me, and I can give it to anyone I want to. So if you worship me, it will all be yours". Jesus answered, "It is written: 'Worship the Lord your God and serve him only'"».

The devil led him to Jerusalem and had him stand on the highest point of the temple. "If you are the Son of God," he said, "throw yourself down from here. For it is written: 'He will command his angels concerning you to guard you carefully; they will lift you up in their hands, so that you will not strike your foot against a stone'". Jesus answered, "It says: 'Do not put the Lord your God to the test'". When the devil had finished all this tempting, he left him until an opportune time».

According to the Gospels, the temptations experienced by Jesus were not, properly speaking, of the moral order. They are proposals the devil makes him so as to mislead him in the way he understands and carries out his mission. So his reaction serves as a model for our moral behavior, but it also warns us not to be misled about the mission Jesus entrusted to his followers.

More than anything else, his temptations help us to recognize, with greater clarity and responsibility, those temptations his church and we who form it may experience. How can we be a church faithful to Jesus if we are not aware of the most dangerous temptations that can lead us astray from his project and his manner of living?

In the first temptation, Jesus refuses to use God to turn stones into bread and satisfy his hunger in this way. He will not take that road. He will not serve his own interests. He will not use the Father to gratify his ego. He will be nourished by the living word of God. He will multiply the loaves of bread only to satisfy the hunger of the people.

Probably the most serious temptation of Christians of rich countries is this: to use religion to add to their material well-being, to sedate their consciences, to drain Christianity of compassion by being deaf to the voice of God who continues to cry out: «*where are your brothers?*»

In the second temptation, Jesus refuses to gain «power and glory» by resorting, as all powerful people do, to the abuses, lies, and injustices which are tools of the devil. The kingdom of God is not imposed on anyone, but offered with love. Jesus will worship only the God of the poor, the weak, and the helpless.

In these times of loss of control over society, it is tempting for the church to attempt to recover the «power and glory» it had in past ages, including an absolute power over society. We are losing an historic opportunity to embark upon a new experiment in humble service and of accompanying men and women today as brothers and sisters much in need of love and hope.

In the third temptation, Jesus refuses to fulfill his mission by having recourse to easy success and self-display. He will not be a triumphant Messiah. He will never put God at the service of his vainglory. He will be among his own as one who serves. It will always be a temptation for some to use the space religion provides to seek reputation, fame and prestige. Few things are as ridiculous in following Jesus as ostentation and seeking to be honored. They harm the church and drain it of the truth.

2
Listen Only to Jesus

«About eight days after Jesus said this, he took Peter, John and James with him and went up onto a mountain to pray. As he was praying, the appearance of his face changed, and his clothes became as bright as a flash of lightning. Two men, Moses and Elijah, appeared in glorious splendor, talking with Jesus. They spoke about his departure, which he was about to bring to fulfillment at Jerusalem.

Peter and his companions were very sleepy, but when they became fully awake, they saw his glory and the two men standing with him. As the men were leaving Jesus, Peter said to him, "Master, it is good for us to be here. Let us put up three shelters —one for you, one for Moses and one for Elijah". (He did not know what he was saying.) While he was speaking, a cloud appeared and enveloped them, and they were afraid as they entered the cloud. A voice came from the cloud, saying,

"This is my Son, whom I have chosen; listen to him". When the voice had spoken, they found that Jesus was alone. The disciples kept this to themselves, and told no one at that time what they had seen».

This scene has traditionally been known as the «Transfiguration of Jesus». We cannot reconstruct with any certainty the experience that gave rise to this astonishing story. We only know the evangelists give it great importance. According to their account, this unique experience allows us to discern something of the real identity of Jesus.

Right at the beginning, the story highlights the transformation of Jesus' face. Even though Moses and Elijah «*appeared in glorious splendor*» to converse with him, perhaps as representatives of the Law and the Prophets respectively, nevertheless, only the face of Jesus remains transfigured and resplendent in the center of the scene.

The disciples have not caught on to the profound meaning of what they are experiencing, for Peter says to Jesus: «*Master, it is good for us to be here. Let us put up three shelters —one for you, one for Moses and one for Elijah*». He places Jesus on the same plane as the great personalities of the Bible: giving to each his shelter. Jesus has not yet secured a central and absolute place in his heart.

The voice of God is about to correct him, revealing to him the real identity of Jesus: «*This is my Son, whom I have chosen*», the one with the transfigured face. He is not to be confused with Moses or Elijah who are in reflected light. «*Listen to him*», and not to anyone else. His word is the only authoritative one. The others have to lead us to him.

The experience of listening to the story of Jesus recounted in the four Gospels had a decisive importance in the church's beginnings within the heart of the Christian communities. We need to recover it today. These four writings constitute for Christians a work we must not equate with the rest of the books of the Bible.

There is something we can find only in the Gospels: it is the impact that Jesus had on the first disciples who felt attracted to him and followed him. The Gospels are not texts that expound academic doctrine about Jesus. Neither are they biographies written to inform us in detail about the history of his life. They are «stories of conversion» calling us to change, follow Jesus, and identify with his project.

3

Were You There?

«*Now there were some present at that time who told Jesus about the Galileans whose blood Pilate had mixed with their sacrifices. Jesus answered, "Do you think that these Galileans were worse sinners than all the other Galileans because they suffered this way? I tell you, no! But unless you repent, you too will all perish. Or those eighteen who died when the tower in Siloam fell on them —do you think they were more guilty than all the others living in Jerusalem? I tell you, no! But unless you repent, you too will all perish".*

Then he told this parable: "A man had a fig tree, planted in his vineyard, and he went to look for fruit on it, but did not find any. So he said to the man who took care of the vineyard, 'For three years now I've been coming to look for fruit on this fig tree and haven't found any. Cut it down! Why should it use up the soil?'

'Sir', the man replied, 'leave it alone for one more year, and I'll dig around it and fertilize it. If it bears fruit next year, fine! If not, then cut it down'"».

Some unknown people came to Jesus and told him about the horrible killing of Galileans in the sacred precincts of the temple. It was Pilate, once again, who had them killed. What shocked them most was that the blood of the murdered men had mingled with that of the animals being sacrificed and offered to God.

We don't know why those people came to Jesus. Did they want him to sympathize with the victims? Did they want him to throw light on what horrendous sin they must have committed to justify such a disgraceful death? If they hadn't sinned, how could God permit a sacrilegious killing in his own temple?

Jesus responded by reminding them of another tragic incident that took place in Jerusalem: the death of eighteen people crushed under the collapse of a tower at the wall close to the pool of Siloam. About both incidents, Jesus makes the same comment: the victims were not guiltier than the other people living in Jerusalem. He concludes with the same warning: «*Unless you repent, you too will perish*».

The answer of Jesus makes us reflect. To begin with, he rejects the traditional belief that all disasters are a punishment of God. Jesus does not think of God as an avenging God, one who goes about punishing his sons and daughters, handing out sicknesses, accidents, or misfortunes here and there in response to their sins.

Later he takes a different approach. He does not develop confusing theories on the ultimate cause of disasters, by attributing them to the guilt of the victims or the providence of God. Jesus turns his attention to those present and confronts them: take all these incidents as a call from God for your conversion, and change your lives.

We are still distressed by the tragic earthquake of Haiti. What light can we shed on this tragedy from the approach of Jesus? Certainly, the first question we should ask is not: Where was God? But rather, where were we? The question that should show us the way to conversion is not: why did God permit such a horrible disaster, but, how can we allow so many human beings to live in unspeakable misery, totally helpless against the forces of nature?

We will not discover the crucified God by demanding an explanation from a distant deity, but by identifying ourselves with the victims. We will not find him by accusing him of indifference or denying his existence, but by working together in a thousand ways to alleviate the suffering in Haiti and in the whole world.

Then, perhaps, we will discern between light and shadows, understanding that God is in the victims, honoring their abiding dignity; and, in those who fight against the catastrophe, God is supporting them in their struggle.

4
The Other Son

«*Now the tax collectors and "sinners" were all gathering around to hear him. But the Pharisees and the teachers of the law muttered, "This man welcomes sinners and eats with them". Then Jesus told them this parable: "There was a man who had two sons. The younger one said to his father, 'Father, give me my share of the estate'. So he divided his property between them.*

"Not long after that, the younger son got together all he had, set off for a distant country and there squandered his wealth in wild living. After he had spent everything, there was a severe famine in that whole country, and he began to be in need. So he went and hired himself out to a citizen of that country, who sent him to his fields to feed pigs.

"He longed to fill his stomach with the pods that the pigs were eating, but no one gave him anything. When he came to his senses, he said, 'How many of my father's hired men have food to spare, and here I am starving to death!' I will set out and go back to my father and say to him: "Father, I have sinned against heaven and against you. I am no longer worthy to be called your son; make me like one of your hired men"».

"So he got up and went to his father. But while he was still a long way off, his father saw him and was filled with compassion for him; he ran to his son, threw his arms around him and kissed

55

him. The son said to him, 'Father, I have sinned against heaven and against you. I am no longer worthy to be called your son'. But the father said to his servants, 'Quick! Bring the best robe and put it on him. Put a ring on his finger and sandals on his feet. Bring the fattened calf and kill it. Let's have a feast and celebrate. For this son of mine was dead and is alive again; he was lost and is found'. So they began to celebrate.

"*Meanwhile, the older son was in the field. When he came near the house, he heard music and dancing. So he called one of the servants and asked him what was going on. 'Your brother has come', he replied, 'and your father has killed the fattened calf because he has him back safe and sound'".*

"*The older brother became angry and refused to go in. So his father went out and pleaded with him. But he answered his father, 'Look! All these years I've been slaving for you and never disobeyed your orders. Yet you never gave me even a young goat so I could celebrate with my friends. But when this son of yours who has squandered your property with prostitutes comes home, you kill the fattened calf for him!'"*

"'*My son', the father said, 'you are always with me, and everything I have is yours. But we had to celebrate and be glad, because this brother of yours was dead and is alive again; he was lost and is found'".*»

This most enduring parable of Jesus, undoubtedly, should be called «the Good Father», but it is wrongly called «the parable of the Prodigal Son». In fact, «the younger son» has always drawn the attention of commentators and preachers. His return home and the incredible welcome of the father have touched every generation of Christians.

The parable, however, also speaks of the older son, a man who stays by his father's side without following the disordered life of his brother, now far from home. Informed of the party thrown by the father for the lost son, he is baffled. Unlike his father, he is not happy his brother has returned. He is furious. «*He became angry and refused to go in*» to join the feasting. He had never left the house, but now he feels a stranger among his own people.

The father goes out to invite him with the same affection with which he had welcomed his brother. He doesn't shout at him or order him. With loving humility he tries to persuade him to take part in the welcoming party. That's when the son loses his temper laying bare his bitterness. He had spent his life doing what his father wanted of him, but he did not learn to love as his father did. All he can do now is to demand his rights and run down his brother.

This is the tragedy of the older son. He had never left the house, but his heart had always been far from home. He knows how to carry out orders but he does not know how to love. He does not understand how his father can still love his lost son. He does not welcome or forgive or want to have anything to do with his brother. Jesus ends his parable without satisfying our curiosity. Did he join the party or stay away?

Caught up in the religious crisis of modern society, we are accustomed to speaking in terms of believers and unbelievers, of practicing and non-practicing Catholics, of marriages blessed by the church and «bad» marriages. We may continue to classify his children, but God keeps waiting for us. He is the property neither of good people nor of practicing Christians. He is the Father of all.

The «older son» is a label for those of us who believe we live close to God. What are we doing, those of us who have not left the church? Are we merely safeguarding our religious survival by observing as well as we can all that is prescribed, or are we witnesses to the great love of God for all his children? Are we building open communities that know how to understand, welcome and accompany those who seek God in spite of doubts and questions? Do we raise barriers or build bridges? Do we regard them with hostility or do we extend the hand of friendship?

The Unknown Revolution

NEITHER DO I CONDEMN YOU

JOHN 8:1-11

FIFTH SUNDAY IN LENT

«*But Jesus went to the Mount of Olives. At dawn he appeared again in the temple courts, where all the people gathered around him, and he sat down to teach them. The teachers of the law and the Pharisees brought in a woman caught in adultery. They made her stand before the group and said to Jesus, "Teacher, this woman was caught in the act of adultery. In the Law Moses commanded us to stone such women. Now what do you say?"*

They were using this question as a trap, in order to have a basis for accusing him. But Jesus bent down and started to write on the ground with his finger. When they kept on questioning him, he straightened up and said to them, "If any one of you is without sin, let him be the first to throw a stone at her". Again he stooped down and wrote on the ground. At this, those who heard began to go away one at a time, the older ones first, until only Jesus was left, with the woman still standing there. Jesus straightened up and asked her, "Woman, where are they? Has no one condemned you?" "No one, sir", she said. "Then neither do I condemn you", Jesus declared. "Go now and leave your life of sin"».

The Pharisees bring before Jesus a woman caught in adultery. Everyone present is aware of her fate. She will be stoned to death according to the Law. No one speaks of the man, her partner. As always in a male dominated society the woman is condemned and the man goes unnamed. The question they pose Jesus is peremptory: «*In the Law Moses commanded us to stone such women. Now what do you say?*»

Jesus does not side with such hypocrisy, which is fueled by male arrogance. That death sentence is not of God. With admirable simplicity and courage he brings truth, justice and compassion to bear on both the trial and the adulteress: *«If any one of you is without sin, let him be the first to throw a stone at her»*. The accusers withdraw in shame. They know very well that they are the ones most responsible for the adulteries committed in that society. Jesus then addresses with respect and tenderness the woman who has just escaped being stoned. He says to her: *«Neither do I condemn you»*. Then he comforts her so that his forgiveness becomes the starting point of a new life: *«Go now and leave your life of sin»*.

That is how wonderful Jesus can be. At last there appears on the earth someone who is not influenced by any law or oppressive power, someone free and big-hearted who has never hated or condemned anyone, who has not returned evil for evil. There is more truth and justice in his defense and forgiveness of the adulteress than in all our bitter demands and condemnations.

Christians have not yet been able to realize and work out all the consequences for women's liberation from oppression that the attitude and practice of Jesus entail. In a church largely led and influenced by males, we fail to become aware of all the injustices women continue to suffer in all spheres of life. One theologian, therefore, spoke about *«the revolution unknown to Christianity»*.

The fact remains that after twenty centuries in supposedly Christian countries, a woman cannot move about freely without a lurking fear of men. Rape, violence, ill-treatment and humiliation are all too real. In fact they are the most deeply rooted forms of violence and cause women the most suffering. Does not the suffering of women have to be reflected far more powerfully and realistically in our liturgical services and find a more important place in our work of social awareness? Do we not, above all, have to be more available to help any and all oppressed women, to denounce abuses and to provide effective protection for them?

6
What Is God Doing on a Cross?

THE NEW COVENANT IN MY BLOOD
LUKE 22:14-23.56
PASSION SUNDAY

«When the hour came, Jesus and his apostles reclined at the table. And he said to them, "I have eagerly desired to eat this Passover with you before I suffer. For I tell you, I will not eat it again until it finds fulfillment in the kingdom of God". After taking the cup, he gave thanks and said, "Take this and divide it among you. For I tell you I will not drink again of the fruit of the vine until the kingdom of God comes".

And he took bread, gave thanks and broke it, and gave it to them, saying, "This is my body given for you; do this in remembrance of me". In the same way, after the supper he took the cup, saying, "This cup is the new covenant in my blood, which is poured out for you. But the hand of him who is going to betray me is with mine on the table. The Son of Man will go as it has been decreed, but woe to that man who betrays him". They began to question among themselves which of them it might be who would do this.

A servant girl saw him seated there in the firelight. She looked closely at him and said, "This man was with him"».

According to the Gospel narrative, those who passed before Jesus crucified on the hill of Golgotha jeered at him and mocking his helplessness said to him: «*If you are the Son of God, come down from the cross*». Jesus did not react to the provocation. His answer is a silence charged with mystery. Precisely because he is the Son of God, he remains on the cross even unto death. Some questions are inevitable. How is it possible for a God to be crucified by men? Do we realize what we are saying? What is God doing on a cross? How can a religion based on such an absurd notion of God survive?

A crucified God amounts to a revolution and a scandal that oblige us to revise our ideas of a God whom we supposedly know. A crucified God has neither the appearance nor the characteristics that all religions attribute to the Supreme Being.

A crucified God is not an all-powerful majestic being, unchangeable and happy, a stranger to our sufferings, but a helpless and humiliated God who suffers pain, anguish and even death with us. Faced with the cross, we either renounce our faith in God or we open our minds to a new and amazing understanding of a God incarnate in our suffering who loves us with a love we will never comprehend.

As we look upon the crucified One, we begin to sense that God, in his mysterious depths, is someone who suffers with us. Our miseries move him. Our sufferings affect him. God is not one who lives, so to say, untouched by our sorrows, tears and misfortunes. God is there at every crucifixion in this world. This crucified God does not admit of a frivolous, selfish faith in an all powerful God who serves our whims and fancies. This God forces us to face the suffering, neglect and abandonment of so many victims of injustice and misfortunes. This is the God we will meet whenever we come close to anyone who is crucified.

Christians will continue to skirt the issue of being faced with a crucified God. We have even learned to look up to the cross of the Lord to avoid looking at those crucified before our very eyes. However, to celebrate the Passion of the Lord in a true spirit we must rekindle our compassion. Without this compassion our faith in the crucified God will run the risk of being false in many ways. When we kiss the cross, let our eyes be fixed on all those close to or far from us who suffer.

Part four

Easter

1

Why Look Among The Dead for Someone Who Is Alive?

HE IS NOT HERE, HE IS RISEN!

LUKE 24:1-12

EASTER

«*On the first day of the week, very early in the morning, the women took the spices they had prepared and went to the tomb. They found the stone rolled away from the tomb, but when they entered, they did not find the body of the Lord Jesus. While they were wondering about this, suddenly two men in clothes that gleamed like lightning stood beside them. In their fright the women bowed down with their faces to the ground, but the men said to them, "Why do you look for the living among the dead? He is not here; he has risen! Remember how he told you, while he was still with you in Galilee: 'The Son of Man must be delivered into the hands of sinful men, be crucified and on the third day be raised again'".*

Then they remembered his words. When they came back from the tomb, they told all these things to the Eleven and to all the others. It was Mary Magdalene, Joanna, Mary the mother of James, and the others with them who told this to the apostles. But they did not believe the women, because their words seemed to them like nonsense. Peter, however, got up and ran to the tomb. Bending over, he saw the strips of linen lying by themselves, and he went away, wondering to himself what had happened».

Faith in Jesus, raised by the Father, did not arise naturally and spontaneously in the hearts of the disciples. Before finding him full of life, the evangelists describe their confusion, their search around the sepulcher, their doubts and uncertainties.

Mary Magdalene is perhaps the best example of what happened to all of them. According to John, she looked for the crucified body of Jesus «*at the first sign of dawn while it was still dark*». Quite naturally, she looks for it «*in the sepulcher*». She does not know that death has been conquered. So the empty tomb leaves her confused. Without Jesus she feels lost.

The other evangelists found another tradition, which describes the search for him by a whole group of women. They cannot forget the Master who received them as disciples. Their love for him leads them to the sepulcher. They do not find Jesus there, but they listen to the message that tells them where to look for him: «*Why do you look for the living among the dead? He is not here. He is risen*».

Faith in the risen Christ does not arise in our hearts spontaneously even today, only because we have learned about it from catechists and preachers. In order to open ourselves out to faith in the resurrection of Jesus we need to make our own spiritual journey. It is all-important not to forget Jesus and to love and seek him passionately with all our energies, but not in the world of the dead. If you are looking for one who is alive, seek him where there is life.

If we want to find the risen Christ full of life and creative power, we must seek him not in a religion that is dead, reduced to fulfilling obligations and external observance of laws and regulations, but instead we must look for him there where the spirit of Jesus is lived, received with faith, love and responsibility toward other followers of Jesus.

We must not seek the risen Christ among Christians divided and clashing among themselves on sterile issues, drained of the love of Jesus and passion for the gospel; instead, we look for him there where they are building communities that place Christ at the center, for they know that «where two or three are gathered in his name, there he will be».

A dull and lifeless Jesus who does not attract us or win our love and who does not touch our hearts or free us is a dead Jesus. He is not the living Jesus, raised by the Father. He is not the one who is alive and gives life.

The One who is alive will not be found in the midst of a stagnant, routine faith, worn out through overuse of themes and formulas void of life experience, but through the seeking of a new quality in our relationship with him and in our identification with his project of bringing about the kingdom of God.

2

Stop Doubting and Believe

Easter

«*Now Thomas (called Didymus), one of the Twelve, was not with the disciples when Jesus came. So the other disciples told him, "We have seen the Lord!" But he said to them, "Unless I see the nail marks in his hands and put my finger where the nails were, and put my hand into his side, I will not believe it".*

A week later his disciples were in the house again, and Thomas was with them. Though the doors were locked, Jesus came and stood among them and said, "Peace be with you!" Then he said to Thomas, "Put your finger here; see my hands. Reach out your hand and put it into my side. Stop doubting and believe". Thomas said to him, "My Lord and my God!"».

The figure of Thomas as the disciple who refuses to believe is well known among Christians. The account in the gospel, nevertheless, says much more about this doubting disciple. The risen Jesus addresses him in words that ring with an urgent call as well as a loving entreaty: «*Stop doubting and believe*». Thomas, who has spent a week resisting believing in the risen Jesus, responds with the most solemn confession of faith we will read about in the Gospels: «*My Lord and My God*».

What has he seen in the risen Lord? What is it that has transformed this up until then doubting and vacillating disciple? What inner search has led him from skepticism to faith?

It is surprising that, according to the account, Thomas does not touch the wounds of Jesus to verify the truth of the resurrection. What draws him to faith is that Jesus himself invited Thomas to touch him.

Through the years we have changed a lot within. We have become more skeptical but also more vulnerable. We have become more critical but also more insecure. We have to decide, each one of us, how we want to live and how we want to die. Each of us has to respond sooner or later to the invitation that may come to us from Jesus either unexpectedly or as a result of a process of inner seeking: «*Stop doubting and believe*».

Perhaps we need to revive our desire to seek the truth, to develop that inner sensitivity we all have to perceive beyond what is visible and tangible: the presence of the Mystery that sustains our lives. It is no longer possible to live as people who know it all; that just is not true. All of us, believers and non-believers, atheists and agnostics, journey through life enveloped in darkness. As Paul of Tarsus says: «*We seek God groping in the dark*».

Why can we not face the mystery of life and death with the faith that love is the ultimate reality of all things? This is the express appeal of Jesus. Many believers today feel that their faith has changed into something increasingly less real and solidly founded. I'm not quite sure why. We know now that we can no longer base our faith on dubious certainties, but we can learn to seek God with more humility and sincerity and without doctrinaire assurances.

Let us not forget that God considers anyone who is a seeker and sincerely wishes to believe, as a believer already. Quite often it is not possible to do much more. And God, who understands our helplessness and weakness, has his own ways to meet each one and offer us salvation. To paraphrase Saint Augustine: We would not seek God if he had not already found us.

3
It Is Not Possible without Easter

FEED MY SHEEP

JOHN 21:1-19

THIRD SUNDAY OF EASTER

«Afterward Jesus appeared again to his disciples, by the Sea of Tiberias. It happened this way: Simon Peter, Thomas (called Didymus), Nathanael from Cana in Galilee, the sons of Zebedee, and two other disciples were together. "I'm going out to fish", Simon Peter told them, and they said, "We'll go with you". So they went out and got into the boat, but that night they caught nothing.

Early in the morning, Jesus stood on the shore, but the disciples did not realize that it was Jesus. He called out to them, "Friends, haven't you any fish?" "No", they answered. He said, "Throw your net on the right side of the boat and you will find some". When they did, they were unable to haul the net in because of the large number of fish.

Then the disciple whom Jesus loved said to Peter, "It is the Lord!" As soon as Simon Peter heard him say, "It is the Lord", he wrapped his outer garment around him (for he had taken it off) and jumped into the water. The other disciples followed in the boat, towing the net full of fish, for they were not far from shore, about a hundred yards.

When they landed, they saw a fire of burning coals there with fish on it, and some bread. Jesus said to them, "Bring some of the fish you have just caught". Simon Peter climbed aboard and dragged the net ashore. It was full of large fish, but even with so many the net was not torn.

Jesus said to them, "Come and have breakfast". None of the disciples dared ask him, "Who are you?" They knew it was the Lord. Jesus came, took the bread and gave it to them, and did the same with the fish. This was now the third time Jesus appeared to his disciples after he was raised from the dead.

> *When they had finished eating, Jesus said to Simon Peter, "Simon son of John, do you truly love me more than these?" "Yes, Lord", he said, "You know that I love you". Jesus said, "Feed my lambs". Again Jesus said, "Simon son of John, do you truly love me?" He answered, "Yes, Lord, you know that I love you". Jesus said, "Take care of my sheep". The third time he said to him, "Simon son of John, do you love me?" Peter was hurt because Jesus asked him the third time, "Do you love me?" He said, "Lord, you know all things; you know that I love you". Jesus said, "Feed my sheep. I tell you the truth, when you were younger you dressed yourself and went where you wanted; but when you are old you will stretch out your hands, and someone else will dress you and lead you where you do not want to go". Jesus said this to indicate the kind of death by which Peter would glorify God. Then he said to him, "Follow me!"».*

The meeting of the risen Jesus with his disciples has a clear catechetical intent. The central symbolism of fishing in the middle of the lake underlies the story. Its message could not be timelier for Christians today: *only the presence of the risen Jesus can make the evangelizing work of the disciples effective.*

To begin with, the story describes the work that the disciples carry out in the darkness of the night. It all begins with the decision of Simon Peter: «*I'm going fishing*». The other disciples are game to go with him. «We'll come with you». They are together again, but Jesus is missing. They go fishing but they embark without being called to do so by him. They only follow the initiative of Simon Peter.

The story writer makes it clear that this work takes place at night and is unsuccessful. «*They caught nothing that night*». «*Night*» means, in the language of the evangelist, the absence of Jesus who is light. Without the presence of the risen Jesus, without his inspiration and his guidance, there is no fruitful evangelization.

Jesus appears with the light of dawn. From the shore he communicates with his people by calling out to them. The disciples are unaware that it is Jesus. They will only recognize him when, obediently following his instructions, they haul in an amazing catch. They owe that only to Jesus, the prophet who earlier one day had called them to be «fishers of men».

The situation of not a few parishes and Christian communities is critical. Their resources are becoming depleted. The most committed Christians must take on multiple tasks and it is always the same people who are called upon to do everything. Have we to intensify our efforts and look for results at any cost, or have we to be more careful to maintain the living presence of the risen Jesus in our work?

In order to spread the Good News of Jesus and to work effectively for his project, it is highly important not to «do many things», but to improve the human and evangelical quality of what we do. The determining factor is not the activities we conduct, but the witness we are called upon to give as Christians.

We cannot restrict ourselves to living a superficial faith. Above all, it is time to care for what is essential. We burden our communities with words, books and writings but what we most need to do is to listen together to Jesus. We have many meetings, but the most important meeting is the one that gathers us together to celebrate the Lord's Supper. He alone can keep filling us with the power to evangelize.

4

Listen to His Voice and Follow His Footsteps

MY SHEEP HEAR MY VOICE ... AND THEY FOLLOW

JOHN 10:27-30

FOURTH SUNDAY OF EASTER

«*"My sheep listen to my voice; I know them, and they follow
me. I give them eternal life, and they shall never perish; no one
can snatch them out of my hand. My Father, who has given them*

to me, is greater than all; no one can snatch them out of my Father's hand. I and the Father are one».

The scene is tense and fraught with conflict. Jesus is walking within the temple precincts. Suddenly a group of Jews surrounds him, harassing him with menace in their looks. Jesus is not intimidated but openly reproaches them for their lack of faith in him. «*You do not believe because you are not my sheep*». The evangelist says that when he finished speaking the Jews took up rocks to stone him.

To prove that they are not his sheep, Jesus makes bold to explain to them what it means to be his sheep. He emphasizes only two characteristics he considers the most essential and indispensable: «*My sheep hear my voice ... and they follow me*». After twenty centuries we Christians need to remember once again that what is essential to be the church of Jesus is to listen to his voice and to follow in his footsteps.

In the first place we must create the ability to listen to Jesus, to develop far more deeply in our communities that sensitivity which is alive in many simple Christians who know how to grasp the Word that comes from Jesus in all its freshness and consonance with the Good News of God. John XXIII said on one occasion that «*the church is like an old village fountain and from its tap cool, fresh water must always flow*». In this twenty-centuries-old church we must see that the cool, fresh water of Jesus keeps flowing.

We live in the midst of a society that invades our consciousness with all kinds of messages, slogans, images, propaganda and claims. If we do not want to see our faith progressively diluted in decadent forms of superficial religiosity, we must learn to place at the center of our communities the living, concrete, unmistakable Word of Jesus, our only Lord.

It is not enough to listen to his voice. We must follow Jesus. The time has come to decide between being satisfied with a «bourgeois religion» that soothes our consciences but stifles our happiness, or to live the Christian faith as a passionate adventure of following Jesus.

The adventure is to believe what he believed, to give importance to what he gave importance to, to defend the dignity of the human person as he defended it; to be with the powerless and vulnerable as he was; to be free to do good as he did; to trust the Father as he trusted him, and to face life and death with the hope with which he faced both.

If those who are lost, lonely or without bearings can find in the Christian community a space where they can learn to live together a life of dignity, solidarity and freedom following Jesus, the church will be offering society one of its best services.

5
Let Us Not Lose Our Identity

LOVE ONE ANOTHER AS I HAVE LOVED YOU

JOHN 13: 31-35

FIFTH SUNDAY OF EASTER

> «*When he was gone, Jesus said, "Now is the Son of Man glorified and God is glorified in him. If God is glorified in him, God will glorify the Son in himself, and will glorify him at once. My children, I will be with you only a little longer. You will look for me, and just as I told the Jews, so I tell you now: Where I am going, you cannot come. A new command I give you: Love one another. As I have loved you, so you must love one another. By this all men will know that you are my disciples, if you love one another"*».

Jesus is bidding his disciples farewell. Within a very short time they will not have him with them. So Jesus speaks to them with special tenderness. «*My children I will be with you only a little longer*». It is a small and vulnerable community. It has just been born. The disciples are like little children. What will become of them without the Teacher?

Jesus makes them a gift: «*A new command I give you. Love one another as I have loved you*». If they love one another with the love with which Jesus has loved them, they will not fail to experience his presence with them. The love that they received from Jesus will continue to spread among them. So Jesus says, «*By this all men will know you are my disciples, if you love one another*».

What will help test whether a community that calls itself Christian truly belongs to Jesus will not be the doctrine it professes or the rites and religious discipline it observes, but the love it manifests that flows from the spirit of Jesus. It is that love that constitutes its identity.

We live in a society where the «culture of exchange» has become increasingly prevalent. People exchange material objects, services and help of every kind. Frequently feelings, bodies and even friendships are self-servingly exchanged. Eric Fromm went so far as to say that «*love is a marginal phenomenon in contemporary society*». People with a capacity for love are the exception.

This analysis is probably too pessimistic. What is certain, however, is that in order to live by the standards of Christian love, it is necessary to resist the culture in which today's society lives. It is not possible to live the love inspired by Jesus without distancing oneself from the kind of relationships and self-serving exchanges that are current among us.

If the influence of the church is being diluted in contemporary society it is not only because of the profound crisis in which religious institutions find themselves. In the case of Christianity, it is also because quite often it is not easy to find in our communities disciples of Jesus, men and women, who excel in their ability to love as Jesus loved. We lack this distinguishing feature of Christian identity.

Christians have talked a lot about love. However we have not dared to or succeeded in investing love with its true meaning based on the spirit and concrete attitudes of Jesus. We have still to learn that Jesus manifested his love in active and creative ways, which led him to being always ready to serve and to struggle against all that dehumanizes people and makes them suffer.

6

Peace in the Church

MY PEACE I GIVE YOU

JOHN 14:23-29

SIXTH SUNDAY OF EASTER

> «Jesus replied, "If anyone loves me, he will obey my teaching. My Father will love him, and we will come to him and make our home with him. He who does not love me will not obey my teaching. These words you hear are not my own; they belong to the Father who sent me. All this I have spoken while still with you. But the Counselor, the Holy Spirit, whom the Father will send in my name, will teach you all things and will remind you of everything I have said to you. Peace I leave with you; my peace I give you. I do not give to you as the world gives. Do not let your hearts be troubled and do not be afraid. You heard me say, 'I am going away and I am coming back to you'. If you loved me, you would be glad that I am going to the Father, for the Father is greater than I. I have told you now before it happens, so that when it does happen you will believe"».

In the Gospel of John we find a collection of discourses of Jesus in which he bids his disciples farewell. Commentators refer to it as the «Farewell Discourse». A special atmosphere surrounds those discourses, for the disciples are afraid of being left without the Master. Jesus, however, insists that despite his departure they will never feel his absence.

He repeats as many as five times that they can count upon the Holy Spirit who will take care of them and keep them faithful to the message and his plan. So calls him «*The Spirit of Truth»*. At one point Jesus gives them a clearer explanation of his mission*: «But the Counselor, the Holy Spirit, whom the Father will send in my name, will teach you all things and will remind you of everything I have said to you»*. This Spirit will be the living memory of Jesus.

The scenario he opens up for the disciples is magnificent. A great spiritual movement of disciples will be born of Jesus and will follow him supported by the Holy Spirit. They will persevere in his truth because the Spirit will keep teaching them everything that he has communicated to them along the roads of Galilee. He will be with them in the future when faced with challenges and temptations to give in to fear.

Jesus wants them to understand well what the Spirit of truth and Advocate of the community will mean to them: *«Peace I leave with you; my peace I give you»*. He does not only wish them peace. He gives them his peace. If they are guided by the Spirit, as they remember and keep his words, they will experience peace.

This is not just any kind of peace. It is his own peace. So he says: *«I do not give to you as the world gives»*. The peace of Jesus is not made up of stratagems involving lies and injustice, but of actions guided by the Spirit of truth. They will find their support in him: *«Do not let your hearts be troubled and do not be afraid»*.

When the church is being discredited and embarrassed in these difficult times, it would be a serious mistake to try to defend our credibility and moral authority by acting without the Spirit of truth promised by Jesus. Fear will keep infiltrating Christianity if we seek to base our security and our peace on means incompatible with the way shown by him.

When the church loses its peace, it is not possible to recover it through just any means or strategy. It is not possible to bring in the peace of Christ while our hearts are full of resentment and blindness. We need humbly to be converted to his truth, to mobilize all our forces in order to retrace our steps from false ways, and to allow ourselves to be guided by the Spirit that inspired the whole life of Jesus.

7

Growth and Creativity

THEY RETURNED TO JERUSALEM WITH GREAT JOY

LUKE 24:46-53

ASCENSION OF OUR LORD

> *«When he had led them out to the vicinity of Bethany, he lifted up his hands and blessed them. While he was blessing them, he left them and was taken up into heaven. Then they worshiped him and returned to Jerusalem with great joy. And they stayed continually at the temple, praising God».*

The Gospels give us several clues for understanding how the first Christian communities began their historic journeys without the presence of Jesus at the head of his followers. Perhaps it was not as simple as we are sometimes led to believe. How did they understand and live their relationship with him once he departed from the earth?

Matthew does not mention his ascension to heaven at all. He ends his Gospel with a farewell scene on a mountain in Galilee where Jesus makes his disciples this solemn promise: *«Surely I am with you always to the very end of the age».* The disciples don't have to feel his absence. Jesus will always be with them, but the question is how this would happen.

Luke has a different setting. In the final scene of his Gospel, *«while he was blessing them, he left them and was taken up into heaven».* The disciples must accept the separation from him in all its reality. Jesus is already living in the mystery of God. But he ascends to the Father while *blessing* his own. His followers begin their historic journey protected by that blessing which Jesus had used to heal the sick, forgive sinners, and caress the little ones.

John the evangelist puts some words in the mouth of Jesus that provide another clue. On bidding his disciples farewell

Jesus says to them, «*I am going to the Father and you are sad…
It is for your good that I am going away. Unless I go away, the
Counselor will not come to you; but if I go, I will send him to you*».
The sadness of the disciples is understandable. They want to
be assured that Jesus will always be with them, but that as-
surance alone would lead to the temptation of staying com-
fortably infantile under the protection of the Master.

The response of Jesus shows a wise method of teaching.
His absence will help the growth of his followers. He leaves
them the mark of his Spirit who, in Jesus' absence, will promote the growth of his own into responsible adulthood. It is
good to remember this, for in these times a fear of creativity,
the temptation to remain stagnant, and nostalgia for a Christianity that is relevant only to a bygone age and culture, seem
to be growing among us.

Throughout history, Christians have fallen into the temptation of following Christ in a childish manner. The historic
presence of Jesus has ended. The Feast of the Ascension reminds us that we are living in the age of the Spirit, the time
for creativity and responsible growth. The Spirit does not
provide the followers of Jesus with «eternal prescriptions».
He gives us light and strength to help us to keep seeking ever
new ways to reproduce the interventions of Jesus. In this way
he leads us to the fullness of the truth of Jesus.

Invocation

I WILL ASK THE FATHER AND HE WILL GIVE YOU ANOTHER
ADVOCATE
JOHN 14:15-16, 23B-26
PENTECOST

«*"If you love me, you will obey what I command. And I will ask
the Father, and he will give you another Counselor to be with
you forever-the Spirit of truth.*

*"If anyone loves me, he will obey my teaching. My Father
will love him, and we will come to him and make our home with
him. He who does not love me will not obey my teaching. These
words you hear are not my own; they belong to the Father who
sent me. All this I have spoken while still with you. But the
Counselor, the Holy Spirit, whom the Father will send in my
name, will teach you all things and will remind you of everything I have said to you"*».

Come Holy Spirit, Creator, and infuse in us the inspiration and
power of Jesus. Without your prompting and grace we will
not succeed in believing in him; we will not have the courage
to follow his footsteps; the church will not be renewed; our
hope will die out. So come and create in us the life-giving
spirit of Jesus.

Come Holy Spirit, and remind us of the inspiring message Jesus gave us. Without your light and witness to him,
we will continue to forget the loving face of God; the gospel
will become a dead letter; the church will not be able to proclaim any good news. So come and teach us to listen only to
Jesus.

Come Spirit of Truth, and make us walk in the truth of Jesus.
Without your light and guidance we will never free ourselves
of our errors and lies; nothing new and true will be born among

us; we will be like the blind who try to guide the blind. So come and make us disciples and witnesses of Jesus.

Come, Spirit of the Father, and teach us to call God «Father», as Jesus did. Without your warmth and your joy, we will live as orphans who have lost their father; we will invoke God with our lips but not with our hearts; our prayers will be empty words. So come and teach us to pray with the words and heart of Jesus.

Come Spirit of Goodness, and convert us to the project of the «kingdom of God» begun by Jesus. Without your power to renew, no one will change our tired hearts; we will not have the courage to build a more humane world following God's will; in your church the last will never be the first; and we will continue in our bourgoise religion. So come and move us to collaborate in the project of Jesus.

Come, Spirit of Love, and teach us to love one another with the love Jesus loved. Without your living presence among us, the communion of the church will collapse; the hierarchy and the people will go on distancing themselves from one another; divisions will increase, dialogue will die out and intolerance will increase. So come and reignite in our hearts and our hands the fraternal love that makes us like Jesus.

Come, Liberating Spirit, and remind us that Christ freed us to be free and to not allow ourselves to be crushed again by slavery. Without your strength and your truth we will not know the love that gives life, but only our selfishness that kills it; the freedom that makes the children of God grow among us will vanish, and we will continue to be victims of fears, cowardice and fanaticism. So come Holy Spirit and create in us the freedom of Jesus.

Part five

Ordinary Time

1
Be Open to the Mystery of God

«"I have much more to say to you, more than you can now bear. But when he, the Spirit of truth, comes, he will guide you into all truth. He will not speak on his own; he will speak only what he hears, and he will tell you what is yet to come. He will bring glory to me by taking from what is mine and making it known to you. All that belongs to the Father is mine. That is why I said the Spirit will take from what is mine and make it known to you. In a little while you will see me no more, and then after a little while you will see me"».

Throughout the centuries, theologians have tried diligently to get to know the mystery of God more intimately. They use different conceptual formulas to describe the relationships that bind and differentiate the divine persons within the Trinity. It is a genuine effort born, no doubt, out of the love and desire for God.

Jesus, however, does not take this approach. Based on his own experience of God, he invites his followers to relate with confidence to God as a Father, to follow faithfully his footsteps as the incarnate Son of God, and to allow themselves to be guided and inspired by the Holy Spirit. This is how he teaches us to be open to the holy mystery of God.

First of all, Jesus calls his followers to live as children of a God who is close to them, who is good and lovable, and whom we can all call upon as a loving Father. What characterizes this Father is not his power and might, but his goodness and infinite compassion. No one is alone. We all have God as a Father who understands us, loves us and forgives us as no one else ever could.

Jesus reveals to us that this Father has a project very close to his heart, born of his love: to build together with all his children a more humane, fraternal, just and inclusive world. Jesus calls it «*the kingdom of God*». He invites all to join this project of the Father who seeks a life of greater justice and dignity for all, beginning with his poorest, most vulnerable and needy children.

At the same time Jesus also appeals to his followers to trust in him: «*Let not your hearts be troubled. You believe in God; believe in me also*». He is the Son of God, the living image of his Father. His words and actions show us how much the Father of all loves us. So he invites everyone to follow him. He will teach us how to live with trust and gentleness in the service of the project of the Father.

With his group of followers, Jesus wants to form a new family in which all seek «*to do the will of the Father*». The legacy he wishes to leave on the earth is this: *a movement of brothers and sisters at the service of the most vulnerable and helpless*. That family will be the symbol and heir of the new world the Father wants.

For that to happen, they will need to receive the Spirit that animates the Father and His Son Jesus: «*You will receive power when the Holy Spirit comes upon you and you will be my witnesses*». This Spirit is the love of God, the breath of life the Father and the Son share, the strength, the drive, and the life-giving energy that will make the followers of Jesus his witnesses and partners at the service of the grand project of the Holy Trinity.

2

The Language of Signs

YOU HAVE SAVED THE BEST TILL NOW

JOHN 2:1-11

SECOND SUNDAY IN ORDINARY TIME

«*On the third day a wedding took place at Cana in Galilee. Jesus' mother was there, and Jesus and his disciples had also been invited to the wedding. When the wine was gone, Jesus' mother said to him, "They have no more wine". "Dear woman, why do you involve me?" Jesus replied. "My time has not yet come".*

His mother said to the servants, "Do whatever he tells you". Nearby stood six stone water jars, the kind used by the Jews for ceremonial washing, each holding from twenty to thirty gallons. Jesus said to the servants, "Fill the jars with water"; so they filled them to the brim. Then he told them, "Now draw some out and take it to the master of the banquet". They did so, and the master of the banquet tasted the water that had been turned into wine. He did not realize where it had come from, though the servants who had drawn the water knew. Then he called the bridegroom aside and said, "Everyone brings out the choice wine first and then the cheaper wine after the guests have had too much to drink; but you have saved the best till now".

This, the first of his miraculous signs, Jesus performed at Cana in Galilee. He thus revealed his glory, and his disciples put their faith in him».

John, the evangelist, does not say that Jesus worked miracles or wonders. He calls them «signs» because they are gestures that point to something deeper than what our eyes can see. Concretely, the signs that Jesus gives lead to his person and reveal his saving power.

What happened at Cana of Galilee is the beginning of all the signs. It is the first example of the kind of signs Jesus will be offering throughout his life. When he transforms water into wine, he places before us the key to understanding the saving transformation that Jesus brings about and his followers must manifest.

Everything takes place within the framework of a wedding. It is the supreme example of human celebration, the most expressive symbol of love, the best image in biblical tradition to evoke the definitive communion of God with a human being. The salvation of Jesus must be lived and presented by his followers as a feast that fulfills the potential of human feasts that are always empty «without wine» and has the capacity to fulfill our desire for total happiness.

The account suggests something more. Water can only be savored as wine when, on the instructions of Jesus, it is «drawn» from six large stone jars used by the Jews for ritual purification. The religion of the law written on tablets of stone lies exhausted. The water in it is incapable of purifying a human being. This religion has to be freed through love and the life Jesus infuses.

We cannot evangelize in any ordinary way. To communicate the transforming power of Jesus, words do not suffice; signs are needed. To evangelize is not only to speak, preach, or teach, and it certainly is not to judge, threaten or condemn. It is necessary to reproduce with creative fidelity the signs Jesus did to bring in the joy of God by making the life of those peasants happier.

Much of the contemporary world remains indifferent to the message of the church. Our liturgical celebrations leave them bored. They need the church to demonstrate signs that touch their lives and are warm and cordial, in order to discover in Christians the capacity of Jesus to alleviate suffering and the hardships of life.

Who would want to listen to what is not presented as joyful news, especially if it is done in the name of the gospel in an authoritarian and menacing manner? Many are waiting for a Jesus who will be their strength and a stimulus for living, and who will show them a more sensible and joyful way to live. If they only know a watered down religion, and do not taste something of the festive joy that Jesus communicated, many will continue to distance themselves from us.

3
In the Same Direction

HE HAS ANOINTED ME TO PREACH GOOD NEWS TO THE POOR

LUKE 1:1-4; 4:14-21

THIRD SUNDAY IN ORDINARY TIME

«Many have undertaken to draw up an account of the things that have been fulfilled among us, just as they were handed down to us by those who from the first were eyewitnesses and servants of the word.

Therefore, since I myself have carefully investigated everything from the beginning, it seemed good also to me to write an orderly account for you, most excellent Theophilus, so that you may know the certainty of the things you have been taught.

Jesus returned to Galilee in the power of the Spirit, and news about him spread through the whole countryside. He taught in their synagogues, and everyone praised him. He went to Nazareth, where he had been brought up, and on the Sabbath day he went into the synagogue, as was his custom. And he stood up to read. The scroll of the prophet Isaiah was handed to him. Unrolling it, he found the place where it is written:

"The Spirit of the Lord is on me, because he has anointed me to preach good news to the poor. He has sent me to proclaim freedom for the prisoners and recovery of sight for the blind, to release the oppressed, to proclaim the year of the Lord's favor".

Then he rolled up the scroll, gave it back to the attendant and sat down. The eyes of everyone in the synagogue were fas-

tened on him, and he began by saying to them, "Today this scripture is fulfilled in your hearing"».

Before he begins to narrate what Jesus did and taught, Luke wants his readers to recognize very clearly the passion that drives the Prophet of Galilee and what the goal of all his activity is. Christians must know the way the Spirit of God led Jesus, for to follow him is to live the same way.

Luke describes in minute detail what Jesus does in the synagogue of his town: he stands up, receives the sacred book, looks for a passage from Isaiah, reads the text, closes the book, returns it and sits down. Everyone needs to listen attentively to the words chosen by Jesus because they explain the task for which he feels sent by God.

Surprisingly, the passage does not speak of organizing a more perfect religion, or a more dignified cult, but of bringing liberation, hope, light and grace to the poorest and the most miserable.

This is what Jesus reads: «*The Spirit of the Lord is on me, because he has anointed me to preach good news to the poor. He has sent me to proclaim freedom for the prisoners and recovery of sight for the blind, to release the oppressed, to proclaim the year of the Lord's favor*». Jesus concludes by saying: «*Today this scripture is fulfilled in your hearing*».

The Spirit of God is in Jesus, sending him to the poor and directing his entire life toward the neediest, the most oppressed and humiliated. It is for this purpose that we, his followers, must work. This is the course God, incarnate in Jesus, wishes to imprint on the history of humanity. The «least» have to be the first to experience a more dignified, liberated and happy life, that God wants from now on for all his children.

We must not forget «the option for the poor». It was not invented by some twentieth century theologians. Nor is it a fad in vogue after the Second Vatican Council. It is the option of the Spirit of God animating the entire life of Jesus. His followers must establish it in human history. Pope Paul vi said:

«It is the duty of the church to help give birth to liberation, and to bring it about in its totality».

It is not possible to live as Jesus lived and make him known if we do not stand by «the lowliest» in solidarity with all who are excluded. If what we as a church of Jesus do and proclaim is not perceived as good and liberating by those who suffer the most, what kind of gospel are we preaching? Which Jesus are we following? What kind of spirituality are we promoting? To come to the point: what impression do we have of the actual church? Are we walking in the footsteps of Jesus?

4
Don't We Need Prophets?

A GREAT PROPHET HAS ARISEN

LUKE 4:21-30

FOURTH SUNDAY IN ORDINARY TIME

> *«All spoke well of him and were amazed at the gracious words that came from his lips. "Isn't this Joseph's son?" they asked. Jesus said to them, "Surely you will quote this proverb to me:'Physician, heal yourself! Do here in your hometown what we have heard that you did in Capernaum"».*
>
> *"I tell you the truth", he continued, "no prophet is accepted in his hometown. I assure you that there were many widows in Israel in Elijah's time, when the sky was shut for three and a half years and there was a severe famine throughout the land. Yet Elijah was not sent to any of them, but to a widow in Zarephath in the region of Sidon. And there were many in Israel with leprosy in the time of Elisha the prophet, yet not one of them was cleansed —only Naaman the Syrian".*

All the people in the synagogue were furious when they heard this. They got up, drove him out of the town, and took him to the brow of the hill on which the town was built, in order to throw him down the cliff. But he walked right through the crowd and went on his way».

«A great prophet has arisen among us». Amazed by the words and deeds of Jesus, this was the cry of people in the villages of Galilee. It is not, however, what happened in Nazareth when he presented himself before his fellow citizens as one anointed a prophet of the poor.

Jesus takes note first of their admiration and then of their rejection of him. He is not taken aback. He reminds them of a well known saying: *«I tell you solemnly, no prophet is ever accepted in his own hometown».* Later when they hustle him out of the town and try to do away with him, Jesus leaves them. The writer reports that he slipped through the crowd and walked away. Nazareth was left without the prophet, Jesus.

Jesus is, and behaves like, a prophet. He is not a priest of the temple, nor is he a teacher of the Law. His life falls within the prophetic tradition of Israel. In contrast to kings and priests, the prophet is not anointed by anyone. His authority comes from God who is bent on inspiring and guiding his beloved people with his Spirit, when political and religious leaders do not know how to do so. It is not accidental that Christians believe in a God incarnate in a prophet.

The characteristics of a prophet are unmistakable. In an unjust society, where the powerful look for their own well-being while silencing the suffering of those who weep, the prophet dares to read and live reality as seen through the compassion of God for the most miserable. His entire life is turned into an «alternative presence» that criticizes injustices and calls for conversion and change.

So, when religion itself comes to terms with an unjust situation and its interests no longer match those of God, the prophet shakes its indifference and self-delusion. He critiques the self-deception that threatens every religion which claims to be everlasting and absolute. He reminds everyone that God alone saves.

A church that ignores the prophetic dimension of Jesus and his followers is in danger of remaining without prophets. We worry about the lack of priests and we pray for vocations to provide priestly ministries. Why do we not pray that God raise up prophets? Don't we need them? Don't we feel the need to develop the prophetic spirit in our communities? Does not a church without prophets run the risk of being deaf to the call of God to conversion and change? Is not Christianity lacking a prophetic spirit open to being controlled by order, tradition or the fear of a God of surprises?

5

Acknowledge Your Sin

LORD, I AM A SINFUL MAN

LUKE 5:1-11

FIFTH SUNDAY ORDINARY TIME

«*One day as Jesus was standing by the Lake of Gennesaret, with the people crowding around him and listening to the word of God, he saw at the water's edge two boats, left there by the fishermen, who were washing their nets. He got into one of the boats, the one belonging to Simon, and asked him to put out a little from shore. Then he sat down and taught the people from the boat.*

When he had finished speaking, he said to Simon, "Put out into deep water, and let down the nets for a catch". Simon answered, "Master, we've worked hard all night and haven't caught anything. But because you say so, I will let down the nets". When they had done so, they caught such a large number of fish that their nets began to break. So they signaled their partners in the other boat to come and help them, and they came and filled both boats so full that they began to sink.

When Simon Peter saw this, he fell at Jesus' knees and said, "Go away from me, Lord; I am a sinful man!" For he and all his companions were astonished at the catch of fish they had taken, and so were James and John, the sons of Zebedee, Simon's partners. Then Jesus said to Simon, "Don't be afraid; from now on you will catch men". So they pulled their boats up on shore, left everything and followed him».

The story of the «miraculous catch of fish» in the lake of Galilee was widespread among the first Christians. Several Gospel writers narrate the episode, but only Luke's story culminates in a moving scene in which the protagonist is Simon Peter, at the same time believer, disciple and sinner. Peter is a man of faith, fascinated by Jesus. His words have more power over him than his own experience. Peter knows that nobody goes to fish in the lake at noon, especially if you have not caught anything at night. But it is Jesus who has told him to do so and Peter trusts him fully, «*Because you say so, I will let down the nets*».

Peter is also a sincere man. Surprised by the huge catch before him, «*he fell at Jesus' knees*» and with admirable spontaneity says, «*Go away from me, Lord, I am a sinful man*». Peter acknowledges before everyone his sinfulness and his utter unworthiness to live close to Jesus.

Jesus is not afraid of having at his side a disciple who is a sinner. On the contrary, if he knows himself to be a sinner, Peter will be able to better understand his message of forgiveness for all, and his welcome to sinners and undesirable people. «*Don't be afraid. From now on you will catch men*». Jesus rids him of the fear of being a disciple who is a sinner and associates him with his mission to gather and call men and women from all walks of life to take part in the saving plan of God.

Why is the church so reluctant to acknowledge its sins and confess its need for conversion? The church belongs to Jesus Christ, but it is not Jesus Christ. It should surprise no one that it has sinned. The church is «holy» because it is sustained and animated by the Spirit of Jesus. But it is «sinful» because it quite frequently resists the Spirit and is unfaithful to the gospel. There is sin in believers and institutions, in the hierarchy and the people of God, in pastors and Christian communities. We all need conversion.

To regularly hide the truth is a very serious matter. It prevents us from engaging in a process of conversion and renewal. Moreover, is not a fragile and vulnerable church, which has the courage to acknowledge its sin, closer to the spirit of the gospel, than an institution needlessly insistent on covering up its miserable failings? Are not our communities more credible when they collaborate with Christ in the task of evangelization by humbly acknowledging their sins and committing themselves to an increasingly more evangelical life? Do we not have much to learn even today from the great apostle Peter, who acknowledged his sinfulness at the feet of Jesus?

6

Take the Poor Seriously

BLESSED ARE THE POOR

LUKE 6:17.20-26

SIXTH SUNDAY IN ORDINARY TIME

«*Looking at his disciples, he said:*

"*Blessed are you who are poor, for yours is the kingdom of God.*
Blessed are you who hunger now, for you will be satisfied.
Blessed are you who weep now, for you will laugh.
Blessed are you when men hate you, when they exclude you and insult you and reject your name as evil, because of the Son of Man.
Rejoice in that day and leap for joy, because great is your reward in heaven. For that is how their fathers treated the prophets.

But woe to you who are rich, for you have already received your comfort.
Woe to you who are well fed now, for you will go hungry.
Woe to you who laugh now, for you will mourn and weep.
Woe to you when all men speak well of you, for that is how their fathers treated the false prophets"».

Accustomed as we are to hearing the Beatitudes just as they appear in the Gospel of Matthew, it becomes very difficult for Christians of rich countries to read the text Luke sets before us. It would seem that the Gospel writer and not a few of his readers belonged to the well-to-do social class. However, far from diluting the message of Jesus he presented a more challenging one.

Together with the blessedness of the poor, the evangelist reminds the rich of the «woes» they incur: «*Blessed are you who are poor … you who hunger now … you who weep now…*». But «*Woe to you who are rich, you who are well fed now… you who laugh now*». Not everyone can listen to the gospel in the same spirit. While it is Good News for the poor, offering them hope, for the rich it is a threat calling them to be converted. How should we listen to this message in our Christian communities?

Jesus first describes the whole brutal reality of the world. It is one the heart of God finds most painful, makes him suffer greatly, and it lies open before his very eyes. It is a reality rich countries try to ignore and to silence time and again. They cover up in a thousand ways the most cruel and inhuman injustices for which we, the rich, must in good measure take the guilt.

Do we want to continue feeding our self-deception or do we want to open our eyes to the reality of the poor? Do we in truth want to do so? Are we going to take seriously some day the vast numbers of those who are undernourished and without dignity of any sort, those who have no voice or power, or those who don't count at all in our onward march toward prosperity?

We Christians have not yet discovered the importance the poor have had in the history of Christianity. More than anyone, they help us to see more clearly our own reality; they disturb our consciences, and permanently call us to conversion. They are the ones who can help us to restructure a church of the future more in keeping with the Gospels. They can make us more humane, more able to be austere, inclusive and generous.

The abyss separating the rich from the poor keeps growing, and it seems to do so relentlessly. In the future, it will be less possible for the church to present itself to the world as the church of Jesus while ignoring the presence of the weakest and the most helpless people on the earth.

Either we take the poor seriously or we forget the Gospels. In rich countries it will be very difficult for us to listen to the word of warning from Jesus: *«You cannot serve God and money»*. It will become unbearable.

7

Without Expecting Anything

DO GOOD… WITHOUT EXPECTING TO GET BACK ANYTHING

LUKE 6:27-38

SEVENTH SUNDAY IN ORDINARY TIME

«"But I tell you who hear me: Love your enemies, do good to those who hate you, bless those who curse you, pray for those who mistreat you. If someone strikes you on one cheek, turn to him the other also. If someone takes your cloak, do not stop him from taking your tunic. Give to everyone who asks you, and if anyone takes what belongs to you, do not demand it back.

"Do to others as you would have them do to you. If you love those who love you, what credit is that to you? Even 'sinners' love those who love them. And if you do good to those who are good to you, what credit is that to you? Even 'sinners' do that. And if

you lend to those from whom you expect repayment, what credit is that to you? Even 'sinners' lend to 'sinners', expecting to be repaid in full.

"But love your enemies, do good to them, and lend to them without expecting to get anything back. Then your reward will be great, and you will be sons of the Most High, because he is kind to the ungrateful and wicked. Be merciful, just as your Father is merciful.

"Do not judge, and you will not be judged. Do not condemn, and you will not be condemned. Forgive, and you will be forgiven. Give, and it will be given to you. A good measure, pressed down, shaken together and running over, will be poured into your lap. For with the measure you use, it will be measured to you".

Why are so many people secretly dissatisfied? Why do so many men and women find life monotonous, trivial, and insipid? Why do they get bored in spite of being financially comfortable? What do they lack to find again the joy of life?

The existence of many would change and acquire another flavor and another life, if they simply learned to love someone *gratis*—for nothing. Like it or not, human beings are made to love unconditionally; and, if they do not do it, a vacuum opens up in their lives that nothing and nobody can fill. It isn't naïve to take seriously the words of Jesus: «*Do good… without expecting to get back anything*». It could turn out to be the secret of a happy life; it could give back to us the joy of life.

It is easy to end life without loving anyone truly gratuitously. I do not harm anyone. I do not interfere in the affairs of others. I respect their rights. I live my life; but can you really call that «life»? Unconcerned about everyone else, confined to my work, my profession, or my trade, insensitive to the problems of others, alien to the sufferings of the people, I shut myself in a «glass ball». What for? To find happiness?

We live in a society where it is difficult to learn to love unselfishly. In almost every case we ask: What's it good for? Is it useful? What do I get in return? We calculate and measure everything. We've become accustomed to the idea that you can get everything by paying for it: food, clothes, housing, transport, entertainment. In this way we run the risk of converting all our interactions into a pure exchange of services.

But love, friendship, acceptance, solidarity, closeness, intimacy, the fight for the weak, hope, inner joy —none of these are obtained with money. They're offered freely without expecting to get back anything, except the growth and enhancement of the life of another.

The first Christians, when speaking of love, used the word *agape* to underline strongly the dimension of grace, over against love that is only understood as *eros,* which could have for many an echo of self-interest and selfishness.

There are men and women in our midst who can only receive love gratuitously, for they hardly have anything to give back to those who wish to come to their aid: people who live alone, those battered by life, misunderstood by almost everyone, impoverished by society, with scarcely any way out in life.

Helder Camara reminds us of the call of Jesus in these words: «*To free yourself of yourself, build a bridge over the abyss of the society your selfishness created. Try to look beyond yourself. Try to listen to another, and, above all, try to make an effort to love instead of loving only yourself*».

8

Be Still

OUT OF THE GOOD STORED IN HIS HEART

LUKE 6:39-45

EIGHTH SUNDAY IN ORDINARY TIME

«*He also told them this parable: "Can a blind man lead a blind man? Will they not both fall into a pit? A student is not above his teacher, but everyone who is fully trained will be like his teacher.*

"Why do you look at the speck of sawdust in your brother's eye and pay no attention to the plank in your own eye? How can you say to your brother, 'Brother, let me take the speck out of your eye', when you yourself fail to see the plank in your own eye? You hypocrite, first take the plank out of your eye, and then you will see clearly to remove the speck from your brother's eye.

"No good tree bears bad fruit, nor does a bad tree bear good fruit. Each tree is recognized by its own fruit. People do not pick figs from thornbushes, or grapes from briers. The good man brings good things out of the good stored up in his heart, and the evil man brings evil things out of the evil stored up in his heart. For out of the overflow of his heart his mouth speaks"».

98 Today our towns and cities provide an atmosphere hardly favorable to those who seek some silence and peace to be with themselves and with God. It is difficult to free oneself from the permanent noise and the constant assault of all kinds of calls and messages. On the other hand, the worries, problems and haste of each day take us from one place to another without allowing us any room to remain masters of ourselves. Not even in one's own house, the scene of frequent tension and the invasion of television, is it easy to find the relaxation and seclusion that are indispensible to rest joyfully in the presence of God.

Paradoxically, in these times when we most need places of silence, solitude, and prayer, believers have abandoned our churches and shrines and we only go to them for Mass on Sundays.

We have forgotten what it means to be still, to interrupt our hurrying for a few minutes, to free ourselves from our tensions for some moments and let quiet and the calm of sacred space permeate our souls. Many men and women are surprised on discovering that frequently it is enough to pause and remain in silence for a time to soothe the spirit and recover clarity and peace. How badly men and women today need this peacefulness to help us enter into contact with ourselves, to regain our freedom, and to release all our inner energy.

Accustomed as we are to noise and talk, we have no idea of the benefits of silence and solitude. We are eager for news, images and impressions. Only that which a person can listen to in the depths of his being is capable of truly nourishing and enriching him. We have forgotten this.

Without this inner peace, one cannot listen to God, recognize his presence in our lives, and grow from within as human beings and believers. According to Jesus, we draw good «*out of the good stored in our hearts*». Good does not arise in us spontaneously. We need to cultivate it and let it build up in the depths of the heart. Many people could begin to change their lives if they succeeded in pausing to listen to the good that God awakens in the stillness of their souls.

9
Humble Faith

I DO NOT DESERVE TO HAVE YOU COME UNDER MY ROOF

LUKE 7:1-10

NINTH SUNDAY IN ORDINARY TIME

> «*When Jesus had finished saying all this in the hearing of the people, he entered Capernaum. There a centurion's servant, whom his master valued highly, was sick and about to die. The centurion heard of Jesus and sent some elders of the Jews to him, asking him to come and heal his servant. When they came to Jesus, they pleaded earnestly with him, "This man deserves to have you do this, because he loves our nation and has built our synagogue".*
>
> *So Jesus went with them. He was not far from the house when the centurion sent friends to say to him: "Lord, don't trouble yourself, for I do not deserve to have you come under my roof. That is why I did not even consider myself worthy to come to*

you. But say the word, and my servant will be healed. For I my-self am a man under authority, with soldiers under me. I tell this one, 'Go', and he goes; and that one, 'Come', and he comes. I say to my servant, 'Do this', and he does it".

When Jesus heard this, he was amazed at him, and turning to the crowd following him, he said, "I tell you, I have not found such great faith even in Israel".

Then the men who had been sent returned to the house and found the servant well».

It is said that all great people are humble, because humility grows in the hearts of all who live their lives sincerely. How much more truthfully can this be said of great believers. No one can have a deep relationship with God unless it is in a modest and humble attitude. How can a person who has in some way experienced God live, except with humility?

Naturally, when the greatness of God has not been ac-knowledged, humility means self-abasement, demeaning oneself—a condition unworthy of being lived.

This is, perhaps, the most profound reason for the pres-ent discrediting of humility in our society. Modern humans are incapable of worshiping the greatness of God; they do not recognize their limitations; they do not sense that their true worth consists in living humbly before God.

The core of all true faith is humility. A beautiful prayer of the liturgy of the church says this: «*Lord, have mercy on us, for we can live neither without you nor with you*». This is what we experience daily. We cannot live without God, and we do not succeed in living with him.

God is light, but, at the same time he's too obscure for us. He is close, but hidden. He speaks to us, but we cannot bear his silence. The believer knows from experience that God is peace, but a peace that causes unease and disquiet. God is purity, but a purity that uncovers our impurity and ugliness.

So everyone who seeks God with sincerity is like the Roman centurion who approached Jesus with these words: «*I do not deserve to have you come under my roof*». Only those who say these words from the depths of their being, and mean them, come to God with truth and dignity.

On the other hand, whoever feels worthy before God behaves unworthily. He is distancing himself from the one who is light and truth. The more we reach into the depths of our hearts, the better we discover that the only way to find God is the way of humility, simplicity and transparency.

Very seldom are we as close to God as when we can recite a prayer like the one L. Boros suggests in one of his works: «*Lord, I have caused much evil in your beautiful world; I have to patiently bear what others are and what I am myself; grant that I may do something so that life may be better wherever you have placed me*».

10
Anesthesia

HE HAD PITY...

LUKE 7:11-17

TENTH SUNDAY IN ORDINARY TIME

> «*Soon afterward, Jesus went to a town called Nain, and his disciples and a large crowd went along with him. As he approached the town gate, a dead person was being carried out —the only son of his mother, and she was a widow. And a large crowd from the town was with her.*
>
> *When the Lord saw her, his heart went out to her and he said, "Don't cry". Then he went up and touched the coffin, and those carrying it stood still. He said, "Young man, I say to you, get up!" The dead man sat up and began to talk, and Jesus gave him back to his mother.*

They were all filled with awe and praised God. "A great prophet has appeared among us", they said. "God has come to help his people". This news about Jesus spread throughout Judea and the surrounding country».

There seems to be an unbelievable need in our society to tragically display human suffering on the front pages of newspapers and on televisions screens. A photograph of a woman weeping over her husband buried in a mine disaster, the image of a hungry child in agony in some Third World country, or of some Palestinians gunned down in their own refugee camp, is worth thousands of dollars.

Every day we read news about the cruelest of happenings and watch images of mass destruction, murders, catastrophes, deaths of innocent victims, as we carry on with our lives without being concerned.

We could say they even give us a «certain feeling of security» because it seems to us those things always happen to others. Our time has not yet come. We can continue to enjoy our weekends and make plans for summer vacations.

When the tragedy is nearer home and the suffering affects someone close to us, we are more disturbed, we don't feel comfortable, and we don't know how to avoid the situation to regain the serenity we lost. Frequently that's exactly what we seek —to recover our little bit of tranquility. At times we pray that hunger and misery would disappear from the world, but simply so that they don't trouble us too much. We wish no one should suffer near us mainly because we don't want to see our daily little happiness endangered.

In a thousand ways we try to avoid suffering, sedate our hearts against the pain others endure, and remain at a distance from everything that can disturb our peace.

The attitude of Jesus tears away our masks, and reveals to us how terribly low our level of humanity has sunk. Jesus is someone who lives each day with profound joy. But his joy is not the fruit of a careful avoidance of suffering —his own or that of others. It has its roots in the joyful experience of God, the Father who welcomes and saves all.

For this reason, his joy is not a sedative that prevents him from being sensitive to the misery around him. When Jesus sees a mother weep over the death of her only son, he does not slip away quietly. He reacts by coming close to the sorrow of the mother as a brother, friend, and sower of peace and life.

In Jesus we keep discovering that believers who have the capacity to enjoy deeply the love of the Father for the lowliest can also suffer with them and alleviate their pain. The one who follows in the footsteps of Jesus will always be a happy person who still misses the happiness of others.

11

Do Not Bar Anyone from Jesus

HER MANY SINS HAVE BEEN FORGIVEN —FOR SHE LOVED MUCH
LUKE 7:36-8:3
ELEVENTH SUNDAY IN ORDINARY TIME

«*Now one of the Pharisees invited Jesus to have dinner with him, so he went to the Pharisee's house and reclined at the table. When a woman who had lived a sinful life in that town learned that Jesus was eating at the Pharisee's house, she brought an alabaster jar of perfume, and as she stood behind him at his feet weeping, she began to wet his feet with her tears. Then she wiped them with her hair, kissed them and poured perfume on them.*

When the Pharisee who had invited him saw this, he said to himself, "If this man were a prophet, he would know who is touching him and what kind of woman she is —that she is a sinner". Jesus answered him, "Simon, I have something to tell you". "Tell me, teacher", he said.

"Two men owed money to a certain moneylender. One owed him five hundred denarii, and the other fifty. Neither of them

had the money to pay him back, so he canceled the debts of both. Now which of them will love him more?" Simon replied, "I suppose the one who had the bigger debt canceled". "You have judged correctly", Jesus said. Then he turned toward the woman and said to Simon, "Do you see this woman? I came into your house. You did not give me any water for my feet, but she wet my feet with her tears and wiped them with her hair. You did not give me a kiss, but this woman, from the time I entered, has not stopped kissing my feet. You did not put oil on my head, but she has poured perfume on my feet. Therefore, I tell you, her many sins have been forgiven —for she loved much. But he who has been forgiven little loves little".

Then Jesus said to her, "Your sins are forgiven". The other guests began to say among themselves, "Who is this who even forgives sins?" Jesus said to the woman, "Your faith has saved you; go in peace".

After this, Jesus traveled about from one town and village to another, proclaiming the good news of the kingdom of God. The Twelve were with him, and also some women who had been cured of evil spirits and diseases: Mary (called Magdalene) from whom seven demons had come out; Joanna the wife of Cuza, the manager of Herod's household; Susanna; and many others. These women were helping to support them out of their own means».

According to Luke's account of the incident, a Pharisee named Simon is very interested in inviting Jesus to a meal with him. Probably he wants to make use of the meal to discuss certain questions with this Galilean who is gaining fame among the people as a prophet. Jesus accepts his invitation: the Good News of God has to reach everyone.

Something takes place during the banquet that Simon has not foreseen. Toward the end of the meal a local prostitute interrupts the proceedings, throws herself at the feet of Jesus and bursts into tears. She does not know how to thank him for the love he shows those who, like her, are held in general contempt. To the surprise of everyone she repeatedly kisses the feet of Jesus and anoints them with an expensive perfume.

Simon watches the scene horrified. A sinful woman touching the feet of Jesus in his own house? He cannot countenance the scandal: this man is unenlightened, not a prophet of God. The unclean woman has to be summarily dragged away from Jesus.

Jesus, however, allows himself to be touched and loved by the woman. She needs him more than anyone else. With special tenderness he offers her God's forgiveness, and then invites her to discover in her heart the humble faith that is saving her. Jesus only wants her to live in peace. «*Your sins have been forgiven. Your faith has saved you. Go in peace*».

All the Gospels highlight the way Jesus accepted and understood the people generally excluded by everyone from God's blessing: prostitutes, tax collectors, lepers. His message caused offense: those despised by the most religious people have a privileged place in the heart of God. There is only one reason for this: they are the ones who stand most in need of acceptance, dignity and love.

The day is approaching when we in Christian communities will have to rethink our attitude toward certain groups in light of how Jesus dealt with them: women who live from prostitution, or homosexuals and lesbians whose problems, suffering and struggles we choose to ignore and suppress at the very heart of the church as if they did not exist.

We need to raise a number of questions: Where can they find among us an acceptance like that of Jesus? From whom can they hear words about God like the ones Jesus spoke to them? What help will they find among us to cope with their sexual orientation responsibly and in consonance with the faith? With whom can they share their faith in Jesus in peace and dignity? Who is able to plumb the depths of the unfathomable love of God for those forgotten by all religions?

12

Do We Believe in Jesus?

WHO DO YOU SAY THAT I AM?

LUKE 9:18-24

TWELFTH SUNDAY IN ORDINARY TIME

> «*Once when Jesus was praying in private and his disciples were with him, he asked them, "Who do the crowds say I am?" They replied, "Some say John the Baptist; others say Elijah; and still others, that one of the prophets of long ago has come back to life". "But what about you?" he asked. "Who do you say I am?" Peter answered, "The Christ of God". Jesus strictly warned them not to tell this to anyone.*
>
> *And he said, "The Son of Man must suffer many things and be rejected by the elders, chief priests and teachers of the law, and he must be killed and on the third day be raised to life". Then he said to them all: "If anyone would come after me, he must deny himself and take up his cross daily and follow me. For whoever wants to save his life will lose it, but whoever loses his life for me will save it"*».

The first Christian generations preserved the memory of this Gospel incident as a story of vital importance to the followers of Jesus. Their instinct was right. They knew that the church of Jesus had to have the question put to it again and again, the one Jesus asked his disciples in the vicinity of Caesarea Philippi: "*Who do you say I am?*»

If in Christian communities we allow our faith in Jesus to die out, we will lose our identity. We will not be able to carry out with creative fearlessness the mission Jesus entrusted to us; we will not dare to face up to the present challenges or remain open to the newness of his Spirit; we will be suffocated in our mediocrity.

Ours are not untroubled times. If we do not return to Jesus more truly and with greater fidelity, our lack of direction will go on paralyzing us; our fine discourses will continue to lose credibility. Jesus is the key, the foundation and the source of all we are, we say and we do. Who is Jesus for Christians today?

We confess, as Peter did, that Jesus is the «Messiah of God», the one *sent* by the Father. This we hold as true: God so loved the world that he gave us Jesus as a gift. Do we Christians know how to accept, care for, enjoy and celebrate this great gift of God? Is Jesus the center of our celebrations, our meetings and gatherings?

We confess him to be the «Son of God». He can teach us to know God better, to trust more in his goodness as a Father, to listen with more faith to his call to build a more fraternal and just world for all. Are we making known in our communities the true face of God incarnate in Jesus? Do we know how to proclaim and communicate him as Good News for all?

We call Jesus «Savior», because he has the power to humanize our lives, to liberate us, and to direct human history toward its true and final salvation. Is this the hope we cherish among us? Is this the peace that spreads out to others from our communities?

We confess that Jesus is our only «Lord». We do not **want** to have other lords, or submit to false idols. But does Jesus truly occupy the center of our lives? Does he hold the absolute first place in our communities? Do we place him above everything and everyone? Do we belong to Jesus? Is he the one who animates and inspires us?

The main task of Christians today is to join forces and to open up ways to reaffirm the central place of Jesus in his church. Everything else flows from this.

13

Without Becoming Established or Looking Back

FOLLOW ME

LUKE 9:51-62

THIRTEENTH SUNDAY

«*As the time approached for him to be taken up to heaven, Jesus resolutely set out for Jerusalem. And he sent messengers on ahead, who went into a Samaritan village to get things ready for him; but the people there did not welcome him, because he was heading for Jerusalem. When the disciples James and John saw this, they asked, "Lord, do you want us to call fire down from heaven to destroy them ?" But Jesus turned and rebuked them, and they went to another village.*

As they were walking along the road, a man said to him, "I will follow you wherever you go". Jesus replied, "Foxes have holes and birds of the air have nests, but the Son of Man has no place to lay his head". He said to another man, "Follow me". But the man replied, "Lord, first let me go and bury my father". Jesus said to him, "Let the dead bury their own dead, but you go and proclaim the kingdom of God". Still another said, "I will follow you, Lord; but first let me go back and say goodby to my family". Jesus replied, "No one who puts his hand to the plow and looks back is fit for service in the kingdom of God"».

To follow Jesus is the very essence of Christian life. Nothing is more important or crucial. It is for this reason that Luke describes three little situations to help the communities reading his Gospel become aware that nothing is more urgent. Following Jesus cannot be delayed.

Jesus uses harsh, even shocking images. It is obvious that he wants to arouse consciences. He is not looking for more followers, but for more committed followers who will follow him unconditionally, giving up false securities and cutting ties they need to sever. His exchanges basically pose one question: what kind of relationship do we, who call ourselves his followers, want to establish with him?

The first scene: One of those accompanying him is so attracted to Jesus that he himself takes the initiative before he is called: *«I will follow you wherever you go».* Jesus makes him aware of the implications of what he is saying: *«Foxes have holes and birds have nests»,* but, *«the son has no place to lay his head».*

It is an adventure to follow Jesus. He does not offer his followers security or well being. He does not help them make money or acquire power. To follow Jesus is to constantly be on the road without becoming established in prosperity or seeking a false refuge in religion. A less powerful and more vulnerable church is not a disaster. It would be the best thing that could happen to us in order to purify our faith and help us put our trust in Jesus.

The second scene: There is another person willing to follow him, but he asks to be allowed to fulfill his sacred obligation *«to bury his father».* This would not come as a surprise to any Jew, for it is one of his most important religious duties. The answer of Jesus is disconcerting: *«Let the dead bury their own dead, but go and proclaim the kingdom of God».*

Finding ways to spread the kingdom of God by working to bring about a more humane way of life is always the most urgent task. Nothing should delay that decision. No one should hold us back or stop us. The *«dead»,* namely, those who are not serving the purposes of the kingdom of life, will devote themselves to other less pressing duties than the coming of the kingdom of God and his justice.

The third scene: To the third man who wishes to bid his family farewell before following him, Jesus says: *«No one who puts his hand to the plow and looks back is fit for service in the kingdom of God».* It is not possible to follow Jesus while looking back. You cannot find ways to spread the kingdom while remaining tied to the past. Working in the project of the Father takes total commitment, trust in a future that is in God's hands, and courage to follow in the footsteps of Jesus.

14
Bearers of the Gospel

THE KINGDOM OF GOD

LUKE 10:1-12, 17-20

FOURTEENTH SUNDAY IN ORDINARY TIME

«*After this the Lord appointed seventy-two others and sent them two by two ahead of him to every town and place where he was about to go. He told them, "The harvest is plentiful, but the workers are few. Ask the Lord of the harvest, therefore, to send out workers into his harvest field. Go! I am sending you out like lambs among wolves. Do not take a purse or bag or sandals; and do not greet anyone on the road. When you enter a house, first say, 'Peace to this house'. If a man of peace is there, your peace will rest on him; if not, it will return to you.*

"Stay in that house, eating and drinking whatever they give you, for the worker deserves his wages. Do not move around from house to house. When you enter a town and are welcomed, eat what is set before you. Heal the sick who are there and tell them, 'The kingdom of God is near you'. But when you enter a town and are not welcomed, go into its streets and say, 'Even the dust of your town that sticks to our feet we wipe off against you. Yet be sure of this: The kingdom of God is near'. I tell you, it will be more bearable on that day for Sodom than for that town".

The seventy-two returned with joy and said, "Lord, even the demons submit to us in your name". He replied, "I saw Satan fall like lightning from heaven. I have given you authority to trample on snakes and scorpions and to overcome all the power of the enemy; nothing will harm you. However, do not rejoice that the spirits submit to you, but rejoice that your names are written in heaven"».

In his Gospel, Luke constructs an important discourse of Jesus that is meant not for the Twelve but for another large group of disciples. He is sending them to work with him in his project of the kingdom of God. The words of Jesus form a kind of founding charter, from which his followers have to find sustenance for their evangelical work.

«*Start off now*». Although we often forget it, the church of Jesus is defined as being *sent by Jesus.* So it is dangerous to think of it as an institution to care for and develop its own religion. The picture of a prophetic movement making its way through history in conformity with the idea of being sent, better matches the original desire of Jesus: it forgets itself, thinks of the welfare of others, presents the Good News of God to the world. «*The Church does not exist for itself, but for humanity*» (Benedict xvi).

Therefore the temptation to withdraw into a shell of our own interests, our past, our doctrinal universe, our rituals and customs is so dangerous today; still worse if we do so by hardening our relation with the world. What kind of church is it that is rigid, stagnant, shut in on itself, without prophets of Jesus, or bearers of the gospel?

«*Whenever you enter into a town … heal the sick who are there and tell them, "The kingdom of God is very near you"*». This is the great news: God is close to us, calling us to make life more humane. We must not stop at announcing the truth so that it becomes attractive and desirable. We need to review our work: What is it today that can draw people to the gospel? How can they perceive God as something new and good?

Evidently, we lack love for the modern world, and we do not know how to reach the hearts of men and women of our times. It is not enough to preach sermons from the altar. We must learn to listen more, to accept people, to heal the lives of those who suffer. Only in this way will we find the right and humble words to bring Jesus to them, this Jesus whose unfathomable tenderness puts us in contact with God, the loving Father of all: «*Whatever house you go into, let your first words be, "Peace to this house"*».

The Good News of Jesus must be communicated with total respect and flow from a loving and friendly approach that conveys peace. It will be a clumsy mistake to try to impose it in an attitude of superiority, threat or resentment. It is against the spirit of the gospel to treat people without love just because they do not welcome our message. Besides, how will they accept it if they do not feel understood by those of us who present ourselves in the name of Jesus?

15
You Do the Same

AND WHO IS MY NEIGHBOR?

LUKE 10: 25-37

FIFTEENTH SUNDAY IN ORDINARY TIME

«But he wanted to justify himself, so he asked Jesus, "And who is my neighbor?"

In reply Jesus said: "A man was going down from Jerusalem to Jericho, when he fell into the hands of robbers. They stripped him of his clothes, beat him and went away, leaving him half dead. A priest happened to be going down the same road, and when he saw the man, he passed by on the other side. So too, a Levite, when he came to the place and saw him, passed by on the other side.

"But a Samaritan, as he traveled, came where the man was; and when he saw him, he took pity on him. He went to him and bandaged his wounds, pouring on oil and wine. Then he put the man on his own donkey, took him to an inn and took care of him. The next day he took out two silver coins and gave them to the innkeeper. 'Look after him', he said, 'and when I return, I will reimburse you for any extra expense you may have'. Which of these three do you think was a neighbor to the man who fell

into the hands of robbers?" The expert in the law replied, "The one who had mercy on him", Jesus told him, "Go and do likewise"».

In order to not lose face in an exchange with Jesus, a teacher of the law ends up asking: «*And who is my neighbor?*», a question only a man concerned about fulfilling the law, would ask. He wants to know whom he should love or exclude from his love. He has no thought for the suffering of people.

Jesus' concern is to alleviate the sufferings of those he meets wherever he goes, breaking, if necessary, the law of the Sabbath or the rules of ritual purity. He answers him with a story vehemently denouncing every kind of religious legalism that exempts one from loving service to those who need it.

On the road going down from Jerusalem to Jericho, a man has been assaulted by bandits. Stripped and despoiled of everything he had, he lies half dead by the roadside, abandoned to his fate. We do not know who he is, except that he is «a man». It could be any of us, any human being laid low by violence, sickness, misfortune, or despair.

It happened that a priest was going down that road. The text emphasizes that it is «by chance», as if a man devoted to worship had no business being there. It isn't his job to come to the aid of the victims left on the roadside. His work place is the temple, the sacred liturgy his duty. When he reaches the spot where the man is lying, he sees him and walks on by, on the other side.

His lack of compassion is not only a personal reaction, because a Levite of the temple who passes by the wounded man does the same thing. It is, more precisely, an attitude and a risk run by those engaged in the world of the sacred: to live far removed from the real world in which people struggle, work and suffer.

When religion is not centered on a God who is a lover of life and Father of those who suffer, sacred worship can become an experience that alienates it from secular life and shields it from direct contact with the suffering of people. It makes us go on with life without reacting when face to face with the wounded we see on the roadside. According to Jesus, it is not those who conduct religious services but those with compassionate hearts who can best show us how to deal with people who suffer.

A Samaritan passes that way. He doesn't come from the temple. He doesn't even belong to the chosen people of Israel. He makes a living as a small trader, a business far removed from anything sacred. But when he sees the wounded man he doesn't ask whether he is a neighbor or not. He is deeply moved and does for him all he can. This is the one we must imitate. That is what Jesus says to the legalistic teacher: «*Go and do likewise*». Whom must we follow when in the normal course of our lives we come across those victims who suffer so deeply because of the economic crisis of our times?

16
Necessary and Urgent

ONLY ONE THING IS NEEDED

LUKE 10:38-42

SIXTEENTH SUNDAY IN ORDINARY TIME

> «*As Jesus and his disciples were on their way, he came to a village where a woman named Martha opened her home to him. She had a sister called Mary, who sat at the Lord's feet listening to what he said. But Martha was distracted by all the preparations that had to be made. She came to him and asked, "Lord, don't you care that my sister has left me to do the work by myself? Tell her to help me!"*
>
> *"Martha, Martha", the Lord answered, "you are worried and upset about many things, but only one thing is needed. Mary has chosen what is better, and it will not be taken away from her"».*

Jesus drops out of a group of disciples on a journey, to enter a village alone. He makes his way to a house where he finds two sisters whom he loves very much. The presence of their friend Jesus will give rise to two very different reactions from the two women.

Mary, almost certainly the younger sister, sets aside everything and remains seated at the feet of the Lord. Her sole concern is to listen to him. The evangelist describes her as having the characteristics of a true disciple: at the feet of the Master, attentive to his voice, absorbing his words, being nourished by his teaching.

The reaction of Martha is different. Since the arrival of Jesus she has been bending over backward to welcome him and to attend to him fittingly. Luke describes her as fretting over all the work she had to do. Pushed beyond her limits and unhappy with her sister, she puts her complaint before Jesus: «*Lord, don't you care that my sister has left me to do all the work by myself? Tell her to come and help me*».

Jesus is unperturbed. He answers Martha with great affection slowly repeating her name; then he makes her see that he too is concerned about the burden of work she bears. But she should know that to listen to him is so important and necessary that no disciple has to be left without his teaching. «*Martha, Martha, you are worried and upset about many things, but only one thing is needed. Mary has chosen what is better, and it will not be taken away from her*». Jesus does not criticize her ministrations. How can he do so when he himself is teaching everyone by his example to welcome, serve, and help others? What he is criticizing is her nervous behavior, under pressure of too much work to do.

Active and contemplative lives are not incompatible for Jesus, and neither are listening faithfully to his Word and being committed to a life of service to others. Rather, he draws attention to the danger of being engrossed in too much activity or being always in inner turmoil. Excess of work and anxiety over it quench the spirit in us, spreading uneasiness and stress more than peace and love.

Under pressure from diminishing resources, we are becoming accustomed to asking the most generous Christians for all kinds of commitments inside and outside the church. If at the same time we do not offer them the time and space to know Jesus, to listen to his Word, and find nourishment in the gospel, we run the risk of increasing anxiety and stress in the church but not making space for Jesus' spirit and his peace. We will find communities kept alive by overburdened staff, but not by witnesses who radiate the spirit and life of the Master.

17

Learn Again to Trust

LORD, TEACH US TO PRAY

LUKE 11:1-13

SEVENTEENTH SUNDAY IN ORDINARY TIME

«One day Jesus was praying in a certain place. When he finished, one of his disciples said to him, "Lord, teach us to pray, just as John taught his disciples". He said to them, "When you pray, say: 'Father, hallowed be your name, your kingdom come. Give us each day our daily bread. Forgive us our sins, for we also forgive everyone who sins against us. And lead us not into temptation".

Then he said to them, "Suppose one of you has a friend, and he goes to him at midnight and says, 'Friend, lend me three loaves of bread, because a friend of mine on a journey has come to me, and I have nothing to set before him'. Then the one inside answers, 'Don't bother me. The door is already locked, and my children are with me in bed. I can't get up and give you anything'. I tell you, though he will not get up and give him the bread because he is a friend, yet because of the man's boldness he will get up and give him as much as he needs.

"So I say to you: Ask and it will be given to you; seek and you will find; knock and the door will be opened to you. For everyone who asks receives; he who seeks finds; and to him who knocks, the door will be opened.

"Which of you fathers, if your son asks for a fish, will give him a snake instead? Or if he asks for an egg, will give him a scorpion? If you then, though you are evil, know how to give good gifts to your children, how much more will your Father in heaven give the Holy Spirit to those who ask him!"».

Luke and Matthew have preserved in their respective gospels some words of Jesus that no doubt remained strongly imprinted in the minds of his closest followers. He probably said them while journeying with his disciples through the villages of Galilee, where they begged something to eat, sought shelter, or knocked at the doors of people.

They likely did not always receive the welcome they expected, but Jesus does not lose heart. His trust in the Father is absolute. His followers have to learn to trust like him: *«Ask and it will be given to you; seek and you will find; knock and the door will be opened to you»*. Jesus knows what he is saying, because this is the experience he had: *«For everyone who asks receives; he who seeks finds; and to him who knocks, the door will be opened»*.

If there is something we must learn again from Jesus in these times of crisis and confusion in his church, it is *trust* —not as an attitude of the naive who comfort themselves hoping for better times, still less as a passive and irresponsible reaction, but as the most evangelical and prophetic behavior in following Jesus the Christ today. In fact even though his three recommendations point to the same basic attitude of trust in God, his language suggests different shades of meaning.

To ask is the proper attitude for the poor who need to receive from another something they cannot obtain by their own effort. This is how Jesus assumed his followers would live: as poor men and women, aware of their weakness and need, without any trace of pride or self-sufficiency. It is not a disgrace to belong to a church that is poor, weak, and stripped of power. What is deplorable is to pretend to follow Jesus today while asking the world for protection that can only come to us from the Father.

To seek is not only to ask. It also requires that we get moving, taking steps to obtain something that is hidden from us because it is covered up or concealed. This is the way that Jesus sees his followers —as seekers of the kingdom of God and his justice. Today we have become accustomed to living in a church that is disconcerted, faced with an uncertain future. The tragedy is that we do not mobilize our forces to seek together new ways to sow the seed of the gospel in modern culture.

To knock at or call out to is to cry out to someone who we feel is not near us, but who, we believe, can hear us and respond. In this way Jesus cried out to the Father from his solitude on the cross. It is understandable that the faith of many Christians who learned to declare, celebrate and live it in a pre-modern culture has grown faint. Sadly, we do not now make enough of an effort to learn to follow Jesus by crying out to God in the midst of the disagreements, conflicts and questions of today's world.

18

Unmask Foolishness

LIFE DOES NOT CONSIST IN THE ABUNDANCE OF POSSESSIONS

LUKE 12:13-21

EIGHTEENTH SUNDAY IN ORDINARY TIME

«*Someone in the crowd said to him, "Teacher, tell my brother to divide the inheritance with me". Jesus replied, "Man, who appointed me a judge or an arbiter between you?" Then he said to them, "Watch out! Be on your guard against all kinds of greed; a man's life does not consist in the abundance of his possessions".*

And he told them this parable: "The ground of a certain rich man produced a good crop. He thought to himself, 'What shall I do? I have no place to store my crops'. "Then he said, 'This is what I'll do. I will tear down my barns and build bigger ones, and there I will store all my grain and my goods. And I'll say to myself, "You have plenty of good things laid up for many years. Take life easy; eat, drink and be merry"'. But God said to him, 'You fool! This very night your life will be demanded from you. Then who will get what you have prepared for yourself?' This is how it will be with anyone who stores up things for himself but is not rich toward God"».

The main character in this little parable of «the foolish rich man» is a landowner like one of those people Jesus knew in Galilee. They were powerful men who mercilessly exploited the peasants, thinking only of how to increase their wealth. People both feared and envied them. Undoubtedly they were counted as being the most fortunate. For Jesus, they were absolutely foolish.

Surprised by a harvest that exceeded his expectations, the rich landowner is now forced to think: *"What shall I do?»* There is no one else in the world of his concerns. He does not seem to have a wife, children, friends or neighbors. He has no thought for the peasants who work his land. He is only concerned about his welfare and his wealth: his harvest, his barns, his property, his life.

The rich man does not realize he is a walled-in human being, a prisoner of a way of thinking that dehumanizes him, stripping him of every vestige of dignity. He only lives to accumulate, to hoard, and to increase his material wealth: *«I will tear down my barns and build bigger ones, and there I will store all my grain and my goods. And I'll say to myself, "You have plenty of good things laid up for many years. Take life easy; eat, drink and be merry"».*

Suddenly, Jesus introduces God himself into the story. His cry interrupts the dreams and fantasies of the rich man: «*You fool! This very night your life will be demanded from you. Then who will get what you have prepared for yourself?*» This is the judgment of God: the life of this rich man is a failure and foolishness. He builds larger barns, but cannot expand the world of his concerns. He increases his wealth, but diminishes and impoverishes his life. He amasses goods, but knows nothing of friendship, generous love, joy, and solidarity. He knows neither how to give nor how to share —only to hoard. Is there anything human about this kind of a life?

The economic crisis we are going through is a *crisis of ambition*: rich countries, big banks, the powerful of the earth have tried to live beyond their means, dreaming of accumulating unlimited wealth, forgetting all the time those sunk in poverty and hunger. But all of a sudden their security has collapsed.

This is not just one more crisis. It is a *sign of the times* that we must interpret in the light of the Gospels. It is not difficult to hear the voice of God in the depths of our consciences: «Enough of so much folly and such cruel neglect of solidarity». We will never overcome our economic crises without a struggle for a profound change in our life style. We must live more austerely. We must share our wealth.

19
We Need them more than Ever

KEEP YOUR LAMPS BURNING

LUKE 12:32-48

NINETEENTH SUNDAY IN ORDINARY TIME

> «*"Do not be afraid, little flock, for the Father has been pleased to give you the kingdom. Sell your possessions and give to the poor. Provide purses for yourselves that will not wear out, a*

treasure in heaven that will not be exhausted, where no thief comes near and no moth destroys. For where your treasure is, there your heart will be also.

"Be dressed ready for service and keep your lamps burning, like men waiting for their master to return from a wedding banquet, so that when he comes and knocks they can immediately open the door for him. It will be good for those servants whose master finds them watching when he comes. I tell you the truth, he will dress himself to serve, will have them recline at the table, and he will come and wait on them. It will be good for those servants whose master finds them ready, even if he comes in the second or third watch of the night.

"But understand this: if the owner of the house had known at what hour the thief was coming, he would not have let his house be broken into. You also must be ready, because the Son of Man will come at an hour when you do not expect him".

Peter asked, "Lord, are you telling this parable to us, or to everyone?" The Lord answered, "Who then is the faithful and wise manager, whom the master puts in charge of his servants to give them their food allowance at the proper time? It will be good for that servant whom the master finds doing so when he returns. I tell you the truth, he will put him in charge of all his possessions. But suppose the servant says to himself, 'My master is taking a long time in coming', and he then begins to beat the menservants and maidservants and to get drunk. The master of that servant will come on a day he does not expect him and at an hour he is not aware of. He will cut him to pieces and assign him a place with the unbelievers.

"That servant who knows his master's will and does not get ready or does not do what his master wants will be beaten with many blows. But the one who does not know and does things deserving punishment will be beaten with few blows. From everyone who has been given much, much will be demanded; and from the one who has been entrusted with much, much more will be asked"».

The first generation of Christians was forced very soon to confront a major problem. The return of the risen Christ was delayed more than expected. The wait was becoming too long for them. How could they keep their hope alive? How could they stop themselves from becoming frustrated, tired, or discouraged?

In the Gospels we find different exhortations, parables, and calls that have only one aim: to keep alive the responsibility of the Christian communities. One of the best known appeals says this: *«Be dressed for service and keep your lamps burning»*. What significance can these words have for us after twenty centuries of Christianity?

The two images are very meaningful. They point to the attitude that servants should have while waiting at night for the master to return: to be prepared to open the door of the house for him as soon as he knocks. They must be ready for action, that is, with tunics drawn up and secured to be able to move and act swiftly. They must have their *«lamps burning»* to keep the house lit up, and for them to remain awake.

Today these words of Jesus are also a call to be awake to reality and to live responsibly without falling into passivity or lethargy. There are times in the history of the church when everything is dark as the night. Nevertheless, those are not the times to put out the lights and go to sleep. They are times to react, to awaken our faith, and to continue our march toward the future, even in a church that has grown old and tired.

One of the major obstacles to propelling the church toward the change it needs is the pervasive passivity of Christians. Unfortunately, during many centuries they have been taught, above all, to be submissive and passive. Even today, it sometimes seems that we do not need Christians to think, plan and promote new ways of being faithful to Jesus Christ.

Hence we should value, take care of, and be grateful for the awakening of a new consciousness in many lay people, men and women, who today live their adherence to Christ and their belonging to the Church with clarity and responsibility. This is, without doubt, one of the most precious fruits of Vatican II, the first Council that dealt directly and explicitly about the importance of the laity as people of God.

Today, such believers can create the ferment that can result in renewed parishes and communities rooted in the faithful following of Jesus. They are the greatest power for change in Christianity. We need them more than ever to build a church open to the problems of the modern world and close to the men and women of today.

20

To Set Fire

I HAVE COME TO BRING FIRE

LUKE 12:49-53

TWENTIETH SUNDAY IN ORDINARY TIME

> «*"I have come to bring fire on the earth, and how I wish it were already kindled! But I have a baptism to undergo, and how distressed I am until it is completed! Do you think I came to bring peace on earth? No, I tell you, but division.*
>
> *From now on there will be five in one family divided against each other, three against two and two against three. They will be divided, father against son and son against father, mother against daughter and daughter against mother, mother-in-law against daughter-in-law and daughter-in-law against mother-in-law"*».

There are many Christians who, strongly established in comfortable social circumstances, have a tendency to regard Christianity as a religion invariably concerned about maintaining the established law and order. The order we frequently uphold, however, is still disorder, because we have not succeeded in feeding the poor, guaranteeing the rights of every person, or even eliminating war or the use of nuclear weapons.

So it is strange to hear sayings from the mouth of Jesus calling not for stability and conservatism, but for a profound change of society: «*I have come to bring fire on the earth, and how I wish it were already kindled!… Do you think I came to bring peace on earth? No, I tell you, but division*».

It is not easy for us to picture Jesus as someone who brings fire to destroy so much impurity, lies, violence and injustice —a Spirit capable of changing the world radically, even at the cost of dividing people and causing them to confront each other.

Believers in Jesus are not fatalists, resigned to their situation, seeking, above all, serenity and peace. They are not reactionaries who justify the way things are, but they work courageously with others for a better world in a creative spirit. Neither are they rebels who, goaded by bitterness, destroy everything to put themselves in the place of those they have brought down.

Whoever understands Jesus lives and acts, moved by a desire and passion to collaborate in a total change. True Christians have revolution in their hearts —a revolution that is not a *coup d'état*, doesn't involve any change of government, civil disorder or political change, but is in fact a search for a more just society.

We need a revolution more profound than economic revolution —a revolution that changes the consciences of human beings and nations. H. Marcuse wrote that we need a world «*in which competition, the struggle of individuals against each other, deceit, cruelty and massacre have no reason to exist*».

Whoever follows Jesus, lives ardently intent on seeing the fire brought by Jesus burn ever more strongly in the world. But Jesis requires, first of all, a radical change in the follower. «*All that is asked of Christians is that they be authentic. This is the real revolution*» *(E. Mounier)*.

21

Not Anything will do

ENTER THROUGH THE NARROW DOOR

LUKE 13:22-30

TWENTY-FIRST SUNDAY IN ORDINARY TIME

125

«Then Jesus went through the towns and villages, teaching as he made his way to Jerusalem. Someone asked him, "Lord, are only a few people going to be saved?" He said to them, "Make every effort to enter through the narrow door, because many, I tell you, will try to enter and will not be able to. Once the owner of the house gets up and closes the door, you will stand outside knocking and pleading, 'Sir, open the door for us'. But he will answer, 'I don't know you or where you come from'. Then you will say, 'We ate and drank with you, and you taught in our streets'. "But he will reply, 'I don't know you or where you come from. Away from me, all you evildoers!'

"There will be weeping there, and gnashing of teeth, when you see Abraham, Isaac and Jacob and all the prophets in the kingdom of God, but you yourselves thrown out. People will come from east and west and north and south, and will take their places at the feast in the kingdom of God. Indeed there are those who are last who will be first, and first who will be last"».

Jesus is traveling toward Jerusalem. His journey is not that of a pilgrim who goes up to the temple to fulfill his religious obligations. According to Luke, Jesus goes through the cities and villages, *«teaching»*. Something needs to be communicated to those people: God is a loving Father who offers his salvation to all. Everyone is invited to receive his forgiveness.

His message surprises everyone. Sinners are full of joy when they hear him speak of the unfathomable goodness of God: even they can hope for salvation. The Pharisees, however, criticize his message and also his welcoming of publicans, prostitutes, and sinners: isn't Jesus opening the way to an unacceptable lessening of religious and moral seriousness?

According to Luke, an unknown person interrupts his journey to ask him about the number of those who will be saved: *Will they be few or many? Will all be saved or only the just?* Jesus does not answer his question directly. It isn't important to know how many will be saved. What matters is to be clear about living in a responsible manner to receive the salvation of a loving God. Jesus reminds all: «*Make every effort to enter through the narrow door*».

In this way he cuts from the root any misunderstanding of his message as an invitation to laxity. For laxity would be ridiculing the Father. Salvation is not something a reckless person receives from a permissive God. Neither is it the privilege of a chosen few. It is not enough to be children of Abraham. It is not enough to have known the Messiah.

It is necessary to strive, to struggle, to imitate the Father, to trust in his forgiveness, and to receive the salvation of God. Jesus does not lower his demands: «*Be compassionate as your Father is compassionate*». «*Do not judge and you will not be judged*». «*Forgive seventy times seven*», as your Father does. «*Seek first the kingdom of God and its justice*».

To understand properly the invitation «*to enter through the narrow door*», we must remember the words of Jesus in the Gospel of John: «*I am the gate; whoever comes in by me will be saved*» (*John 10:9*). To enter through the narrow door is to follow Jesus: to learn to live like him; to take up his cross and trust in the Father who raised him from the dead.

When we follow Jesus, we can't do just anything we wish. We must respond faithfully to the love of the Father. What Jesus asks is not scrupulous observance of the law, but radical love of God and neighbor. Therefore, his call is a source of responsibility, but not of anguish. Jesus is always an open door. No one can close it. It is we who shut ourselves off from his forgiveness.

22
Without Expecting Anything in Return

DO NOT TAKE THE PLACE OF HONOR

LUKE 14:1, 7-14

TWENTY-SECOND SUNDAY IN ORDINARY TIME

«*One Sabbath, when Jesus went to eat in the house of a prominent Pharisee, he was being carefully watched. When he noticed how the guests picked the places of honor at the table, he told them this parable: "When someone invites you to a wedding feast, do not take the place of honor, for a person more distinguished than you may have been invited. If so, the host who invited both of you will come and say to you, 'Give this man your seat'. Then, humiliated, you will have to take the least important place. But when you are invited, take the lowest place, so that when your host comes, he will say to you, 'Friend, move up to a better place'. Then you will be honored in the presence of all your fellow guests. For everyone who exalts himself will be humbled, and he who humbles himself will be exalted".*

Then Jesus said to his host, "When you give a luncheon or dinner, do not invite your friends, your brothers or relatives, or your rich neighbors; if you do, they may invite you back and so you will be repaid. But when you give a banquet, invite the poor, the crippled, the lame, the blind, and you will be blessed. Although they cannot repay you, you will be repaid at the resurrection of the righteous"».

Jesus is seated at table with one of the leading Pharisees of the region who had invited him for a meal. Luke suggests that the Pharisees continued to spy on him. But Jesus feels free to criticize the guests who were looking for the first places and even to suggest to his host those whom he should invite in the future.

These instructions given to the host leave us confused. In clear and simple language, Jesus tells him how to behave: «*Do not invite your friends, your brothers, relatives or your rich neighbors*». But is there anything more permissible and natural than to strengthen ties with people who wish us well? Didn't Jesus do the same with Lazarus, Martha and Mary, his friends in Bethany?

At the same time Jesus points out to him those who should be included: «*Invite the poor, the crippled, the lame, the blind*». The poor do not have the means to return the favor when invited. Nothing can be expected from the crippled, the lame and the blind. So no one invites them. Isn't this something we all quite normally, inevitably do?

Jesus does not reject love of the family or friendly relations. What he does not accept is that those relations regularly claim priority and become privileged and exclusive. Jesus reminds those who enter the dynamics of the kingdom of God, seeking a more human and fraternal world, that acceptance of the poor and the forsaken has to take precedence over relations based on self-interest and social compromise.

Is it possible to live in a disinterested manner? Can we love without expecting anything in return? We have strayed so far from the Spirit of Jesus, that often even friendship and family love are a trade-off. Let us not deceive ourselves. The way of gratitude is almost always long and difficult. It is necessary to learn things like this: to give without expecting much in return; to forgive without requiring recompense; to be patient with disagreeable people; to help while looking only for the good of the other.

It is always possible to cut down on our own interests; to sometimes give up little advantages; to put joy in the life of someone in need; to give away some of our time without keeping it always to ourselves; to work with others in small freely given services.

Jesus makes bold to say to the Pharisee who invited him: «Blessed are you if they cannot repay you». This beatitude has been so long forgotten that many Christians have never heard it spoken. Nevertheless it contains a message Jesus loved very much: «Blessed are those who live for others without any recompense. The Heavenly Father will reward them».

23
Responsible Realism

ESTIMATE THE COST

LUKE 14:25-33

TWENTY-THIRD SUNDAY IN ORDINARY TIME

«*Large crowds were traveling with Jesus, and turning to them he said: "If anyone comes to me and does not hate his father and mother, his wife and children, his brothers and sisters —yes, even his own life— he cannot be my disciple. And anyone who does not carry his cross and follow me cannot be my disciple.*

"Suppose one of you wants to build a tower. Will he not first sit down and estimate the cost to see if he has enough money to complete it? For if he lays the foundation and is not able to finish it, everyone who sees it will ridicule him, saying, 'This fellow began to build and was not able to finish'.

"Or suppose a king is about to go to war against another king. Will he not first sit down and consider whether he is able with ten thousand men to oppose the one coming against him with twenty thousand? If he is not able, he will send a delegation while the other is still a long way off and will ask for terms of peace.

In the same way, any of you who does not give up everything he has cannot be my disciple"».

Jesus may use different examples, but his teaching is the same: whoever undertakes a major project rashly without first examining whether he has the resources and the ability to achieve what he wants, runs the risk of failure. No farmer sets himself to build a tower to protect his vineyards without first spending some time to work out whether he will be able to complete the job successfully. Otherwise the project will remain unfinished, prompting his neighbors to make fun of him. No king decides to go to battle against a powerful enemy without previously determining whether the battle will end in victory or suicide.

At first it looks as if Jesus is encouraging prudent and cautious behavior, so markedly different from the boldness he expects from his own. Nothing could be further from the truth. The mission that Jesus is entrusting to his disciples is so important that no one should commit himself to it unthinkingly, rashly or imprudently.

His warning takes on great relevance in these times of crisis, so decisive for the future of our faith. Jesus invites us, first of all, to reflect in the mature manner in which the two protagonists of the parables «*sit down*» to reflect. It would be highly irresponsible today for the disciples of Jesus not to know what they want; what they want to achieve; and what resources they need to attain their purpose.

When will we sit down to join forces, reflect together, and cooperatively devise the plan we need to follow? Do we not need to set aside more time, to listen more to the message of the gospel, and to meditate more on it in order to discover new callings, promote charisms and develop a new way to follow Jesus?

Jesus also warns us to be realistic. We are going through an unprecedented socio-cultural change:

- *Is it possible to spread the faith in this new world being born, without knowing it well and understanding it from within?*
- *Is it possible to help people gain an understanding of the gospel if we do not know how men and women today think and feel, or if we do not understand the language they speak?*
- *Is it not a mistake to respond to the challenges of today with dated, irrelevant policies?*

It would be foolish in the present crisis to act blindly and unthinkingly. We would expose ourselves to failure, frustration and even ridicule. As the parable warns, an unfinished tower would only invite the contempt of people toward the builder. We must not forget the realistic and humble words of Jesus inviting his disciples to become the leaven in the midst of people, or salt to bring a new flavor to the lives of all.

24
A Parable for Today

⤱

I WILL GO BACK TO MY FATHER

LUKE 15:1-32

TWENTY-FOURTH SUNDAY IN ORDINARY TIME

«*Jesus continued: "There was a man who had two sons. The younger one said to his father, 'Father, give me my share of the estate'. So he divided his property between them.*

"Not long after that, the younger son got together all he had, set off for a distant country and there squandered his wealth in wild living. After he had spent everything, there was a severe famine in that whole country, and he began to be in need. So he went and hired himself out to a citizen of that country, who sent him to his fields to feed pigs. He longed to fill his stomach with the pods that the pigs were eating, but no one gave him anything.

"When he came to his senses, he said, 'How many of my father's hired men have food to spare, and here I am starving to death! I will set out and go back to my father and say to him: 'Father, I have sinned against heaven and against you. I am no longer worthy to be called your son; make me like one of your hired men'.

"So he got up and went to his father. But while he was still a long way off, his father saw him and was filled with compassion for him; he ran to his son, threw his arms around him and kissed

him. The son said to him, 'Father, I have sinned against heaven and against you. I am no longer worthy to be called your son'.

"*But the father said to his servants, 'Quick! Bring the best robe and put it on him. Put a ring on his finger and sandals on his feet. Bring the fattened calf and kill it. Let's have a feast and cele brate. For this son of mine was dead and is alive again; he was lost and is found'. So they began to celebrate.*

"*Meanwhile, the older son was in the field. When he came near the house, he heard music and dancing. So he called one of the servants and asked him what was going on. 'Your brother has come', he replied, 'and your father has killed the fattened calf because he has him back safe and sound'.* "*The older brother became angry and refused to go in. So his father went out and pleaded with him. But he answered his father, 'Look! All these years I've been slaving for you and never disobeyed your orders. Yet you never gave me even a young goat so I could celebrate with my friends. But when this son of yours who has squandered your property with prostitutes comes home, you kill the fattened calf for him!' 'My son', the father said, 'you are always with me, and everything I have is yours. But we had to celebrate and be glad, because this brother of yours was dead and is alive again; he was lost and is found'*"».

In no other parable did Jesus want to have us enter so profoundly into the mystery of God and of the human condition. No other parable is as contemporary for us as the one of the Father who loves.

The younger son says to his father: «*Give me my share of the estate*». In claiming it, he is in some way asking for his father's death. He wants to be free, to break all ties, but he will not be free until his father passes away. His father gives in to his wish without a word: for the son must freely choose his future.

Isn't this the same situation we are in? Many want to be free of God, to be happy, uninhibited by an eternal Father on their horizon. God has to disappear from society and from our consciences. And just as in the parable, the Father remains silent. God does not bring pressure on anyone.

The son leaves for «*a distant country*». He needs to live in another region, far from his father and his family. The father sees him go, but does not leave him. The heart of a father goes with him; every morning he waits for him. Modern society is withdrawing more and more from God, from his authority, from the memory of him. But isn't God following us even while we lose sight of him?

Soon the son takes to a life of «*wild living*», which suggests not only a morally disordered life, but also an insane, messy and chaotic existence. In a short time his adventure becomes a drama. A terrible hunger overtakes him, and he only survives by herding swine as a slave for an unknown man. His own words reveal his tragedy: «*Here I am starving to death*».

We have a void within us, and the hunger for love can be the first sign of our distance from God. Freedom isn't child's play. What is it we lack? What is it that can fill our hearts? We have all we want, so what is it we hunger for?

The young man «*came to his senses*», and entering deeply into the emptiness within, remembered the face of his father that reflected an abundance of food: in the house of my father «*they have food to spare and here I am starving to death*». There grows in him a desire for a new freedom close to his father. He recognizes his blunder and makes a decision: «*I will set out and go back to my father*».

Will we take the road to God our Father? Many would if they knew the God who according to the parable of Jesus, «*ran to meet his son, threw his arms around him, and kissed him*». Those arms and kisses speak of the Father's love better than all the books of theology. At his side we could discover a more honorable and joyful freedom.

25

Money

YOU CANNOT SERVE BPTH GOD AND MONEY

LUKE 16:1-13

TWENTY-FIFTH SUNDAY IN ORDINARY TIME

«Jesus told his disciples: "There was a rich man whose manager was accused of wasting his possessions. So he called him in and asked him, 'What is this I hear about you? Give an account of your management, because you cannot be manager any longer'. The manager said to himself, 'What shall I do now? My master is taking away my job. I'm not strong enough to dig, and I'm ashamed to beg —I know what I'll do so that, when I lose my job here, people will welcome me into their houses'. So he called in each one of his master's debtors. He asked the first, 'How much do you owe my master?' 'Eight hundred gallons of olive oil', he replied. The manager told him, 'Take your bill, sit down quickly, and make it four hundred'. Then he asked the second, 'And how much do you owe?' 'A thousand bushels of wheat', he replied. He told him, 'Take your bill and make it eight hundred'.

"The master commended the dishonest manager because he had acted shrewdly. For the people of this world are more shrewd in dealing with their own kind than are the people of the light. I tell you, use worldly wealth to gain friends for yourselves, so that when it is gone, you will be welcomed into eternal dwellings.

"Whoever can be trusted with very little can also be trusted with much, and whoever is dishonest with very little will also be dishonest with much. So if you have not been trustworthy in handling worldly wealth, who will trust you with true riches? And if you have not been trustworthy with someone else's property, who will give you property of your own? No servant can serve two masters. Either he will hate the one and love the other, or he will be devoted to the one and despise the other. You cannot serve both God and Money"».

The society Jesus lived in was quite different from ours. The only families able to accumulate gold and silver coins were the powerful big land owners of Tiberias. The peasants could hardly acquire even the bronze or copper coins that were of little value. Many lived by exchanging products in a subsistence economy without the use of money.

In this society Jesus spoke of money with surprising frequency. He had no land or fixed work. So his life as an itinerant prophet dedicated to the cause of God allowed him to speak with complete freedom. His love for the poor and his passion for God's justice compel him always to defend the most excluded.

When he speaks of money, he chooses a very personal language. He forthrightly calls it «unjust money» or «unjust riches». He's never seen «clean money». The wealth of those powerful people is unjust because it has been amassed unjustly. Moreover, they enjoy it without sharing it with the poor and the hungry.

What can those who possess these unjust riches do? Luke has preserved a strange saying of Jesus. The condensed phrase may be somewhat obscure; its content must not be allowed to be forgotten. «*I tell you, use worldly wealth to gain friends for yourselves so that when it is gone, you will be welcomed into eternal dwellings*».

In effect, Jesus says to the rich: «Use your unjust money to help the poor; win their friendship by sharing with them your goods. They will be your friends. At the hour of death, money will no longer be of use to you. Then they will welcome you into the house of the Father». In other words, the best way to launder unjust money in the eyes of God is to share it with the poorest of his children.

The people received his words with scorn. Luke tells us that when the Pharisees heard all this they sneered at Jesus, because they loved money. They do not understand the message of Jesus. They are not interested in hearing him speak of money. They are only concerned about knowing and observing the Law faithfully. They consider wealth a sign of God's blessing on their lives.

Although a long biblical tradition reinforces this view of wealth as a blessing, *it is not true to the gospel of Jesus.* Let me say this loud and clearly, because there are rich people who think, almost as a matter of course, that economic success and prosperity are clear evidence of God's favor. The truth is that a follower of Jesus may not do anything he pleases with money. Making money, spending and enjoying it is unjust if it forgets the poorest.

26

Don't Ignore Those Who Suffer

A BEGGAR NAMED LAZARUS

LUKE 16:19-31

TWENTY-SIXTH SUNDAY IN ORDINARY TIME

« *"There was a rich man who was dressed in purple and fine linen and lived in luxury every day. At his gate was laid a beggar named Lazarus, covered with sores and longing to eat what fell from the rich man's table. Even the dogs came and licked his sores. The time came when the beggar died and the angels carried him to Abraham's side. The rich man also died and was buried.*

"In hell, where he was in torment, he looked up and saw Abraham far away, with Lazarus by his side. So he called to him, 'Father Abraham, have pity on me and send Lazarus to dip the tip of his finger in water and cool my tongue, because I am in agony in this fire'. But Abraham replied, 'Son, remember that in your lifetime you received your good things, while Lazarus received bad things, but now he is comforted here and you are in agony. And besides all this, between us and you a great chasm has been fixed, so that those who want to go from here to you cannot, nor can anyone cross over from there to us'. He answered, 'Then I beg you, father, send Lazarus to my father's house, for I

have five brothers. Let him warn them, so that they will not also come to this place of torment'. Abraham replied, 'They have Moses and the Prophets; let them listen to them'. 'No, father Abraham', he said, 'but if someone from the dead goes to them, they will repent'. He said to him, 'If they do not listen to Moses and the Prophets, they will not be convinced even if someone rises from the dead'"».

The contrast between the two central characters in the parable is tragic. The rich man dresses in purple and fine linen. His whole life is a story of luxury and ostentation. He exudes the glow of an effortless hedonism. All he thinks of everyday is partying splendidly. This rich man is nameless because he has no identity; he is a nobody. His life, devoid of compassion, is a fiasco. No one can live only on partying.

At the entrance of his mansion there lies a hungry beggar covered with sores. No one helps him. Just a few dogs come near to lick his wounds. He has nothing except a name that carries hope with it. His name is Lazarus, «Eliezer», which means, «God is my help».

At death their fortunes change radically. The rich man is buried, of course with full pomp, but is taken to *hades*, the kingdom of the dead. Lazarus also dies. There is no mention of a funeral rite for him, but «*angels carried him to Abraham*». Using images everyone in his day easily understood, Jesus reminds everyone that God has the last word over rich and poor.

The rich man is not considered an exploiter. No one denounced him as an impious man cut off from the Covenant. Quite simply, he enjoyed his riches and ignored a poor man. The man was stretched out in front of his eyes, but he did not see him. He lay at his doorstep, but he didn't meet him. He excluded him from his life. His was a sin of indifference.

Sociologists tell us that apathy and lack of sensitivity toward the suffering of others is growing in society. In a thousand ways we avoid noticing the way people suffer. Little by little we become incapable of seeing their plight.

The sight of a beggar on our way annoys us. It disturbs us to meet a friend suffering from a terminal disease. We don't know what to do or say. It is better to stay away; get back to our business; keep from being touched by it.

It is much easier to cope with suffering that takes place far away from us. We have learned to reduce hunger, misery or sickness to data, numbers and statistics. They analyze the reality but hardly touch our hearts. We know how to watch horrible suffering on television, but on the screen it is always unreal and less terrifying. When grief or pain affects someone close to us, we try in a thousand ways to deaden our feelings.

Those who follow Jesus become more sensitive to the sorrow of anyone they come across. They go to meet a person in need, and if they can, they try to ease that person's situation.

27
Increase Our Faith

FAITH AS SMALL AS A MUSTARD SEED

LUKE 17:5-10

TWENTY-SEVENTH SUNDAY IN ORDINARY TIME

«*The apostles said to the Lord, "Increase our faith!" He replied, "If you have faith as small as a mustard seed, you can say to this mulberry tree, 'Be uprooted and planted in the sea', and it will obey you. Suppose one of you had a servant plowing or looking after the sheep. Would he say to the servant when he comes in from the field, 'Come along now and sit down to eat'? Would he not rather say, 'Prepare my supper, get yourself ready and wait on me while I eat and drink; after that you may eat and drink'? Would he thank the servant because he did what he was told to do? So you also, when you have done everything you were told to do, should say, 'We are unworthy servants; we have only done our duty'"*».

All of a sudden the disciples make Jesus an important request of Jesus: «*Increase our faith*». On another occasion they had asked him: «*Teach us to pray*». As Jesus begins to reveal to them God's plan, the task he wants to entrust to them, the disciples come to feel that their faith, nurtured from childhood, does not suffice to help them to respond to his call. They need a more robust and vigorous faith.

Twenty centuries have gone by. Throughout history the followers of Jesus have seen years of fidelity to the gospel as well as dark hours of infidelity, times of strong faith and times of crisis and uncertainty. Do we not need to ask the Lord to increase our faith?

Lord, increase our faith! Teach us that faith does not consist in believing something but in believing in you, incarnate Son of God. Open our hearts to your Spirit; let your Word break through to us; may we learn to live the way you did and to follow closely in your footsteps. You are the only one who awakens our faith and finally crowns it.

Increase our faith! Give us a faith focused on what is essential, purified of accretions and spurious additions that draw us away from the core of the gospel. Teach us to live in these difficult times with a faith not based on external supports, but on your living presence in our hearts and in our communities of believers.

Increase our faith! Give us a stronger life-giving relationship with you, knowing you, our Teacher and Lord, are the most important, the best, the most precious and beautiful of everything we have in the church. Give us a radiant faith that will lead us to a new phase in Christianity, more faithful to your Spirit and to the course you traced.

Increase our faith! Help us to identify ourselves with the project of the kingdom of God, working together in concrete ways and with conviction to make life more humane just as the Father wants it. Help us to live our faith humbly with passion for God and passion for every human being.

Increase our faith! Teach us to make the change to a life more true to the gospel. Let us not resign ourselves to a watered down Christianity. Let not the salt lose its savor, nor let the church lose alarmingly its quality of a leaven in society. Awaken in us the faith of the apostles and prophets.

Increase our faith! Let us not deteriorate into a Christianity without the cross. Teach us to discover that faith does not consist in believing in a God who suits us, but in one who strengthens our responsibility and expands our capacity to love. Teach us to follow you by taking up our cross each day.

Increase our faith! Let us experience your risen presence among us as you renew our lives and inspire our communities.

140

28

Healing

HE CAME BACK, PRAISING GOD

LUKE 17:11-19

TWENTY-EIGHTH SUNDAY IN ORDINARY TIME

«Now on his way to Jerusalem, Jesus traveled along the border between Samaria and Galilee. As he was going into a village, ten men who had leprosy met him. They stood at a distance and called out in a loud voice, "Jesus, Master, have pity on us!" When he saw them, he said, "Go, show yourselves to the priest". And as they went, they were cleansed. One of them, when he saw he was healed, came back, praising God in a loud voice. He threw himself at Jesus' feet and thanked him —and he was a Samaritan. Jesus asked, "Were not all ten cleansed? Where are the other nine? Was no one found to return and give praise to God except this foreigner?" Then he said to him, "Rise and go; your faith has made you well"».

This incident is well known. Jesus heals ten lepers while sending them to the priests to have them certified as cured and returned to their families. The account could have ended there, but the evangelist is keen on highlighting how one of them reacted.

Once cleansed, the lepers vanish from the scene. We do not hear any more of them. It seems they were untouched by what had happened to them. One of them, however, «*saw that he was healed*» and realized that something extraordinary had been given him. God has healed him. He returns, praising God in a loud voice and giving thanks to Jesus.

Most commentators interpret his reaction as an act of gratitude: the other nine are an ungrateful lot; he is the only one who returned to show gratitude. That is what the account seems to suggest. Jesus, however, does not speak of gratitude. He says the Samaritan returned «*to give praise to God*». To give such praise and glory to God is much more than to give thanks.

Each of us has a personal history of trials from sickness, suffering and hardships. Within each history, healing is a privileged event for giving praise and glory to God as the Savior of our being. Saint Irenaeus of Lyon expressed it famously: «*The glory of God is man fully alive*». The body of the leper now restored to health, sings of the glory of God.

We claim to know everything about how our bodies function, but we are still surprised when we are cured of a serious illness. It is always a mystery how we go through the experience of recovering from an illness and see how we regain strength and recover our confidence and our freedom.

There are very few experiences as radical and basic as healing, for in healing we experience victory over evil, the triumph of life over the danger of death. When we recover we are offered the possibility of accepting God in a new way. He comes to us as the ground of our being and the source of new life.

Modern medicine allows people today to undergo the process of healing more frequently than in times past, and we should thank those who heal us. Healing can also be an occasion for and a stimulus to a new relationship with God. We can change from indifference to faith, from rejection to acceptance, from doubt to trust, from fear to love.

This healthy acceptance of God can heal us from fears, emptiness, and wounds that harm us. It can create the foundation for a life of greater health and freedom. It can heal us totally.

29

The Cry of Those Who Suffer

WILL NOT GOD BRING ABOUT JUSTICE?

LUKE 18:1-8

TWENTY-NINTH SUNDAY IN ORDINARY TIME

> «Then Jesus told his disciples a parable to show them that they should always pray and not give up. He said: "In a certain town there was a judge who neither feared God nor cared about men. And there was a widow in that town who kept coming to him with the plea, 'Grant me justice against my adversary'. For some time he refused. But finally he said to himself, 'Even though I don't fear God or care about men, yet because this widow keeps bothering me, I will see that she gets justice, so that she won't eventually wear me out with her coming!' And the Lord said, "Listen to what the unjust judge says. And will not God bring about justice for his chosen ones, who cry out to him day and night? Will he keep putting them off? I tell you, he will see that they get justice, and quickly. However, when the Son of Man comes, will he find faith on the earth?"».

The parable of the widow and the unscrupulous judge, an open story like many others, can elicit different reactions from listeners. Luke says it is a call to pray without losing heart. But it is also an invitation to trust in God who will do justice to those who cry out to him day and night. What reaction does this dramatic incident evoke in us today since it reminds us of countless victims unjustly abandoned to their fate?

In biblical tradition the widow is the supreme example of a person who is alone and helpless. This woman has no husband or children to protect her; no one to support or back her. All she has are opponents to exploit her and a judge without religion or a conscience, who cares nothing for the suffering of anyone.

What the complainant asks is nothing fanciful. All she demands is justice. This is her repeated and firm protest before the judge: «*Grant me justice*». Her demand is that of all those unjustly oppressed. It is a cry in keeping with what Jesus says to his followers: «*Seek the kingdom of God and his justice*».

It is true that God has the last word and will do justice to those who cry to him day and night. This is the hope inspired in us by Christ raised to life by the Father from an unjust death. But until that day arrives, the cries grow from those who keep calling out without anyone heeding them.

For a great majority of the world's population life is a never ending night of waiting. Religions promise salvation. Christianity proclaims the triumph of the love of God incarnate in Jesus crucified. Meanwhile millions of people know only the hardness of heart of their fellow human beings and the silence of God. Often, we believers are the ones who hide the face of the Father veiling it with our religious selfishness.

Why does our discourse with God not prompt us to heed at last the cry of those who suffer injustice and appeal to us in a thousand ways: «Give us justice»? If, when we pray, we are truly in God's presence, why are we not able to hear more clearly the insistent demands for justice that reach the heart of the Father?

This parable challenges all believers. Will we continue to nurture our private devotions while forgetting those who suffer? Will we go on praying to God to put him at the service of our interests without bothering about the injustices in the world? What if to pray meant precisely to forget ourselves and to seek, with God, a more just world for all?

30

The Right Attitude

HE WHO HUMBLES HIMSELF WILL BE EXALTED

LUKE 18:9-14

THIRTIETH SUNDAY IN ORDINARY TIME

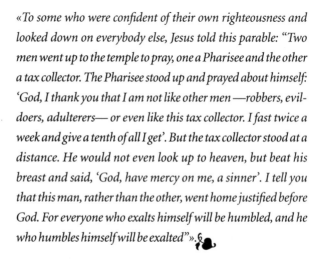

«To some who were confident of their own righteousness and looked down on everybody else, Jesus told this parable: "Two men went up to the temple to pray, one a Pharisee and the other a tax collector. The Pharisee stood up and prayed about himself: 'God, I thank you that I am not like other men —robbers, evildoers, adulterers— or even like this tax collector. I fast twice a week and give a tenth of all I get'. But the tax collector stood at a distance. He would not even look up to heaven, but beat his breast and said, 'God, have mercy on me, a sinner'. I tell you that this man, rather than the other, went home justified before God. For everyone who exalts himself will be humbled, and he who humbles himself will be exalted"».

According to Luke, Jesus spoke this parable to some people who prided themselves on being virtuous and despised everyone else. The two leading characters who go up to the temple to pray represent two contrasting and irreconcilable religious attitudes. But which is the proper and right attitude before God? This is a matter of serious concern.

The Pharisee is a scrupulous observer of the Law, a faithful follower of his religion. He is comfortable in the temple. He stands with head erect, confident of how good and great he is.

It is easy to see that something is wrong with this prayer. Rather than pray, this man indulges in self-glorification. He is boasting about his own life-story. He needs to feel righteous before God by showing himself superior to everyone else.

This man doesn't know what it means to pray. He is not aware of the mysterious greatness of God, and neither does he recognize how small he himself is. It is stupid to come into the presence of God in order to enumerate our own good works and to despise others. This is the prayer of an atheist that is concealed beneath a cloak of piety. This man does not need God, does not ask him anything, nor does he need anyone.

The publican's prayer is very different. He knows his presence in the temple isn't at all well regarded. The business he does as a tax collector is hated and despised. He has no defense. He is aware that he is a sinner. His beating his breast and the few words he mumbles say it all: «*God, have mercy on me, a sinner*».

This man is aware that he has nothing to boast about, nothing to offer God, but much to receive from him: God's forgiveness and mercy. His prayer is honest and sincere. He is a sinner, but he is on the path to truth.

The Pharisee did not find a way to God. This tax collector, on the other hand, immediately finds the right attitude toward God —the attitude of one who has nothing but needs everything. He doesn't even pause to confess his failings in detail. He recognizes he is a sinner. His prayer is born of that awareness: «*Have mercy on me, a sinner*».

The two go up to the temple to pray, but each one is moved by an idea of God that he has in his mind, and he relates to God accordingly. The Pharisee remains caught up in a legalistic religion: for him, it is important to be righteous in God's eyes and to be more observant than anyone else. The tax collector on the other hand, opens himself to the God of love that Jesus preaches. He has learned to accept the forgiveness and love of God in his life without boasting of anything or condemning anyone.

31

Can I Change?

TO SAVE WHAT WAS LOST

LUKE 19:1-10

THIRTY-FIRST SUNDAY IN ORDINARY TIME

«*Jesus entered Jericho and was passing through. A man was there by the name of Zacchaeus; he was a chief tax collector and was wealthy. He wanted to see who Jesus was, but being a short man he could not, because of the crowd. So he ran ahead and climbed a sycamore-fig tree to see him, since Jesus was coming that way. When Jesus reached the spot, he looked up and said to him, "Zacchaeus, come down immediately. I must stay at your house today".*

So he came down at once and welcomed him gladly. All the people saw this and began to mutter, "He has gone to be the guest of a 'sinner'". But Zacchaeus stood up and said to the Lord, "Look, Lord! Here and now I give half of my possessions to the poor, and if I have cheated anybody out of anything, I will pay back four times the amount". Jesus said to him, "Today salvation has come to this house, because this man, too, is a son of Abraham. For the Son of Man came to seek and to save what was lost"».

Luke narrates the incident of Zacchaeus for his readers to help them better discover what they can expect of Jesus: the Lord whom they call upon and follow in Christian communities «*has come to seek and to save what was lost*».

At the same time, his account of the behavior of Zacchaeus helps to answer the question many ask themselves: Can I still change? Isn't it too late for me to undo the past I have largely wasted? What steps should I take?

The characteristics with which Zacchaeus has been described clearly portray his life. He is «*chief tax collector*» and he is «*wealthy*». *Everyone in Jericho knows he is a sinner* —a man who does not serve God but money.

Zacchaeus, however, is anxious to see Jesus. He isn't prompted by curiosity, but wants to know who Jesus is and what this prophet has that attracts great crowds of people. It isn't easy for one established in his way of life. But this desire to see Jesus is going to change his life. The man will have to get past several hurdles. He is a «*short man*», but more importantly, he is not motivated by lofty ideals. People are another obstacle: he will have to overcome social prejudices. These barriers will make a personal, serious meeting with Jesus difficult.

But Zacchaeus pursues his search with simplicity and sincerity. He runs ahead of the crowd and climbs a tree like a child. He doesn't think of his dignity as an important person; he only looks for the right time and place to meet Jesus. He wants to see him.

He soon discovers that Jesus too is seeking him. For when Jesus reaches the spot, he looks up and says to him: «*Zacchaeus, come down immediately. I must stay at your house today*». Zacchaeus climbs down and welcomes him with unbounded joy. There are decisive times when Jesus passes by in our lives, for he wants to save what we are losing. We must not miss them.

Luke doesn't describe the meeting. He speaks of the transformation of Zacchaeus, who changes the way he sees life. He no longer thinks only of his money, but also of the suffering of others. He changes the way he lives; he will do justice to those he has exploited and share his possessions with the poor.

Sooner or later we all run the risk of establishing ourselves in a set way of life and of giving up any desire for a higher human quality of life. A more genuine encounter with Jesus, we believers must realize, can make our lives more humane and, above all, more inclusive.

32

For God, His Children Do Not Die

TO HIM ALL ARE ALIVE

LUKE 20:27-38

THIRTY-SECOND SUNDAY IN ORDINARY TIME

«*Some of the Sadducees, who say there is no resurrection, came to Jesus with a question. "Teacher", they said, "Moses wrote for us that if a man's brother dies and leaves a wife but no children, the man must marry the widow and have children for his brother. Now there were seven brothers. The first one married a woman and died childless.*

"The second and then the third married her, and in the same way the seven died, leaving no children. Finally, the woman died too. Now then, at the resurrection whose wife will she be, since the seven were married to her?" Jesus replied, "The people of this age marry and are given in marriage. But those who are considered worthy of taking part in that age and in the resurrection from the dead will neither marry nor be given in marriage, and they can no longer die; for they are like the angels. They are God's children, since they are children of the resurrection.

"But in the account of the bush, even Moses showed that the dead rise, for he calls the Lord 'the God of Abraham, and the God of Isaac, and the God of Jacob'. He is not the God of the dead, but of the living, for to him all are alive"».

Jesus has always been very serious when speaking about new life after the resurrection. However, when a group of aristocratic Saducees tries to ridicule faith in the resurrection of the dead, Jesus reacts by raising the issue to a level of seriousness making two basic statements.

To begin with, Jesus rejects the childish idea of the Sadducees who imagine the life of those raised from the dead as a continuation of this life as we know it now. It is a mistake to speak of life resurrected by God in terms of our earthly experience. There is a radical difference between our life on earth and the fullness of life sustained directly by the love of God after death. That life is absolutely new. Hence we can hope for it, but never describe or explain it.

The first generations of Christians maintained this humble and honest attitude to the mystery of «eternal life». Paul told the believers of Corinth they were dealing with something *«no eye has seen, no ear has heard, no mind has conceived what God has prepared for those who love him»*.

These words serve as a healthy warning and a joyful expectation. Heaven is something so totally new that no earthly experience can compare with it; it is a life prepared by God to completely fulfill our deepest longings. It is the function of faith not to naively satisfy our curiosity, but to nourish the desire and hope placed in God.

This is precisely what Jesus is seeking when he appeals in all simplicity to a fact the Sadducees accept: in the biblical tradition God is referred to as the God of Abraham, Isaac and Jacob. Even though these patriarchs are dead, God continues to be their God, protector and friend. Death has not been able to destroy the love and faithfulness of God toward them.

Jesus draws his own conclusion while making an important statement for our faith: *«God is not the God of the dead, but of the living; because to him they are all alive»*. God is an inexhaustible source of life. Death does not leave God without his beloved sons and daughters. Even as we mourn their loss on this earth, God sees them sparkle with life because he holds them in the embrace of a Father's faithful love.

According to Jesus, the relationship of God with his children cannot be destroyed by death. His love is more powerful than our biological extinction. So we dare to call upon him with humble faith: *«In you I trust. O my God, do not let me be put to shame»* (Psalm 25:1-2).

33

In Testing Times

BY STANDING FIRM YOU WILL GAIN LIFE

LUKE 21:5-19

THIRTY-THIRD SUNDAY IN ORDINARY TIME

«*Some of his disciples were remarking about how the temple was adorned with beautiful stones and with gifts dedicated to God. But Jesus said, "As for what you see here, the time will come when not one stone will be left on another; every one of them will be thrown down".*

"Teacher", they asked, "when will these things happen? And what will be the sign that they are about to take place?" He replied: "Watch out that you are not deceived. For many will come in my name, claiming, 'I am he', and, 'The time is near'. Do not follow them.

"When you hear of wars and revolutions, do not be frightened. These things must happen first, but the end will not come right away". Then he said to them: "Nation will rise against nation, and kingdom against kingdom. There will be great earthquakes, famines and pestilences in various places, and fearful events and great signs from heaven. But before all this, they will lay hands on you and persecute you. They will deliver you to synagogues and prisons, and you will be brought before kings and governors, and all on account of my name. This will result in your being witnesses to them.

"But make up your mind not to worry beforehand how you will defend yourselves. For I will give you words and wisdom that none of your adversaries will be able to resist or contradict. You will be betrayed even by parents, brothers, relatives and friends, and they will put some of you to death. All men will hate you because of me. But not a hair of your head will perish. By standing firm you will gain life"».

Profound socio-cultural changes are taking place in our times, and a religious crisis is shaking the foundations of Christianity in the West. These happenings should, more than ever, urge us to seek from Jesus the light and strength we need to discern and face them in an intelligent and responsible way.

What is happening is a call to realism. Jesus never promises his followers an easy road to success and glory. On the contrary, he makes it clear that all along, their history will be full of difficulties and struggle. To foster triumphalism or nostalgia for grandeur of any kind is against the spirit of Jesus. This way of life, which seems extraordinarily hard to us, is most in keeping with a church faithful to its Lord.

Let us not be naive. In times of crisis, disagreement, and confusion it is not unusual that messages and revelations proposing new ways to salvation are propagated. These are the watchwords of Jesus: «*Take care not to be deceived*». Do not be foolish enough to believe teachings alien to the gospel, either from within or outside the church.

Refuse to join them. Do not follow those who take us away from Jesus, the only foundation and source of our faith.

Let us focus on what is essential. Every Christian generation has its own problems, difficulties, and needs. We must not lose our serenity, but assume responsibility for ourselves. We are not asked anything beyond our strength. We can count on the help of Jesus himself: «*I will give you words and wisdom*». Even in an atmosphere of rejection and ill-will, we can practice the gospel and live with Christian wisdom and common sense.

This is a time for witnessing. Hard times should not be a reason for lamenting, nostalgia, or discouragement. It is not the time for resignation, passivity, or quitting. Jesus sees things differently: in crises «*this will result in your being witnesses to them*». This is precisely when we must rise to the need to become humble but convincing witnesses of Jesus, of his message and of his project.

Let us have patience. The recommendation of Jesus for difficult times is this: *«By standing firm you will gain life».* The original term can be translated either as «patience» or «perseverance». We Christians speak little of patience, but we need it more than ever. It is time to develop a Christian, patient, and tenacious way of life that will help us to respond to new situations and challenges without losing our peace or the clarity of our vision.

34
Carrying the Cross

152 THIS IS THE KING OF THE JEWS

LUKE 23:35-43

CHRIST THE KING

> *«The people stood watching, and the rulers even sneered at him. They said, "He saved others; let him save himself if he is the Christ of God, the Chosen One". The soldiers also came up and mocked him. They offered him wine vinegar and said, "If you are the king of the Jews, save yourself". There was a written notice above him, which read:* THIS IS THE KING OF THE JEWS. *One of the criminals who hung there hurled insults at him: "Aren't you the Christ? Save yourself and us!" But the other criminal rebuked him. "Don't you fear God", he said, "since you are under the same sentence? We are punished justly, for we are getting what our deeds deserve. But this man has done nothing wrong". Then he said, "Jesus, remember me when you come into your kingdom". Jesus answered him, "I tell you the truth, today you will be with me in paradise"».*

The story of the crucifixion, solemnly read on the feast of Christ the King, reminds us, as followers of Jesus, that his kingdom is not a kingdom of glory and power, but of service, love and total commitment to saving human life from evil, sin and death.

Accustomed as we are to proclaiming the victory of the cross, we run the risk of forgetting that the crucified Christ has nothing to do with a false triumphalism that renders meaningless the sublime act of humble service of God to his creatures. The cross is not a trophy we proudly display to others, but a symbol of the crucified love of God inviting us to follow the example of Jesus.

We praise, worship and kiss the cross of Christ because in the depths of our being we feel the need to give thanks to God for his boundless love. But we can't forget that the first thing Jesus insistently asks of us is not to kiss the cross but to carry it. This means following in his footsteps in a responsible and committed manner. Sooner or later we know it will lead us to share his painful destiny.

We are not to approach the mystery of the cross in a disinterested way, with no intention of carrying it. Great care is needed to make sure religious services concerning the cross do not create an attractive but dangerous atmosphere. For it may draw us away from faithfully following the crucified Christ, falsely assuming we can live as Christians without the cross. We mut hear the call of Jesus when we kiss the cross: «*If someone wishes to come after me, let him take up his cross and follow me*».

For the followers of Jesus to lay claim to the cross is to be with the crucified of society in a spirit of service: seeking justice where the helpless are abused, and calling for compassion where there is only indifference toward those who suffer. For this we will experience conflicts, rejection and suffering, but it will be our humble way of carrying the cross of Christ.

The Catholic theologian, Johann Baptist Metz, insists there is a danger that the image of the crucified Jesus may be hiding from us the face of those who are being crucified today. According to him, a very serious phenomenon is taking place in Christianity in prosperous countries: «*The Cross does not disturb anyone any more. It has lost its impact. It has lost the eagerness it inspired of following Jesus; it does not appeal to our sense of responsibility; rather it releases us from it*».

Do we not all need to re-examine our real attitude toward the crucified Christ? Do we not need to relate to him with greater dedication and responsibility?

Other Feasts

1

Remember Jesus!

THEY ALL ATE AND WERE SATISFIED

LUKE 9:11-17

THE HOLY BODY AND BLOOD OF CHRIST

«But the crowds learned about it and followed him. He welcomed them and spoke to them about the kingdom of God, and healed those who needed healing. Late in the afternoon the Twelve came to him and said, "Send the crowd away so they can go to the surrounding villages and countryside and find food and lodging, because we are in a remote place here". He replied, "You give them something to eat".

They answered, "We have only five loaves of bread and two fish —unless we go and buy food for all this crowd". (About five thousand men were there.) But he said to his disciples, "Have them sit down in groups of about fifty each". The disciples did so, and everybody sat down.

Taking the five loaves and the two fish and looking up to heaven, he gave thanks and broke them. Then he gave them to the disciples to set before the people. They all ate and were satisfied, and the disciples picked up twelve basketfuls of broken pieces that were left over».

As they narrated the story of the Last Supper of Jesus with his disciples, the first generations of Christians would remember the solemnly expressed desire of the Master: «*Do this in memory of me*». This is how Luke and Paul, the evangelizer of the gentiles, look back on it.

Ever since it began, the supper of the Lord has been celebrated by Christians in memory of Jesus, to make his living presence a reality in our midst, and to nourish our faith in him, in his message and in his life given for us unto death. Let us recall the four most significant moments in the present structure of the Mass. The thoughtful participation of the community highlights the meaning of these moments and the way to live them.

Listening to the gospel. We remember Jesus when we listen to the story of his life and his message in the Gospels. They were written specifically to preserve the memory of Jesus and thus strengthen the faith and the will of his disciples to follow him.

We do not infer any doctrine from the Gospel narrative but we learn, above all, that the way Jesus was and acted should be a model and inspiration for the way we live. So we must listen to it with the attitude of disciples who wish to learn to think, feel, love, and live like him.

The memory of the Supper. We remember the saving act of Jesus as we listen with faith to the words: «*This is my body. See me in these pieces of bread giving myself for you even unto death. This is the cup of my blood. I have shed it for the forgiveness of your sins. Thus you will remember me always. I have loved you to the full extent of my love*».

At this time we confess our faith in Jesus Christ in this synthesis of the mystery of our salvation: «*We announce your death, we proclaim your resurrection. Come, Lord Jesus*». We are overjoyed that we are saved by Christ, our Lord.

The Prayer of Jesus. Before communion, we recite the prayer Jesus taught us. First we identify with the three great desires close to his heart: his absolute respect for God, the coming of his kingdom of justice, and the fulfillment of the will of the Father. Next we make our own the four petitions to the Father: bread for all, forgiveness and mercy, overcoming of temptation, and deliverance from all evil.

Communion with Jesus. We come, like the needy human beings we are, with outstretched hands; we take the bread of life, receiving it with an act of faith; in silence we welcome Jesus in our hearts and in our lives. «*Lord, I want to live in communion with you, to follow your footsteps, to be animated by your spirit, and to collaborate with you in your project to build a more compassionate world*».

2
Faithful Follower of Jesus

THE MOTHER OF MY LORD

LUKE 1:39-56

ASSUMPTION OF OUR LADY

«At that time Mary got ready and hurried to a town in the hill country of Judea, where she entered Zechariah's home and greeted Elizabeth. When Elizabeth heard Mary's greeting, the baby leaped in her womb, and Elizabeth was filled with the Holy Spirit. In a loud voice she exclaimed: "Blessed are you among women, and blessed is the child you will bear! But why am I so favored, that the mother of my Lord should come to me? As soon as the sound of your greeting reached my ears, the baby in my womb leaped for joy. Blessed is she who has believed that what the Lord has said to her will be accomplished!"

And Mary said: "My soul glorifies the Lord and my spirit rejoices in God my Savior, for he has been mindful of the humble state of his servant. From now on all generations will call me blessed, for the Mighty One has done great things for me —holy is his name. His mercy extends to those who fear him, from generation to generation. He has performed mighty deeds with his arm; he has scattered those who are proud in their inmost thoughts. He has brought down rulers from their thrones but has lifted up the humble. He has filled the hungry with good things but has sent the rich away empty. He has helped his servant Israel, remembering to be merciful to Abraham and his descendants forever, even as he said to our fathers". Mary stayed with Elizabeth for about three months and then returned home».

The evangelists describe Our Lady with features that should reignite our devotion to Mary, the Mother of Jesus. Their portrayal of her helps us to love and imítate her, to medítate on her life, pray to her and have confidence in her with a new and more evangelical spirit.

Mary is the great believer, the first follower of Jesus, the woman who knew how to ponder in her heart the deeds and words of her Son. She is the prophet who sings to God the savior of the poor, glorifying him. She is the faithful mother who remains by the side of her persecuted Son, condemned to death and executed on the cross. She is the witness of the risen Christ, who receives, together with the disciples, the Spirit who will always be with the church of Jesus. Luke, for his part, invites us to make the hymn of Mary our own, to let ourselves be guided by her zeal for Jesus. For in the Magnificat the faith of Mary shines out in all its splendor, as does also her maternal identification with her Son, Jesus.

Mary begins by proclaiming the greatness of God: «*My spirit rejoices in God, my Savior, for he has been mindful of the humble state of his handmaid*». God is bountiful to the lowly. Mary praises God with the same joy with which Jesus blessed the Father, because he has hidden himself from the «wise and the learned» and has revealed himself to the lowly. The faith of Mary in the God of the «lowly» helps us resonate with the mind and heart of Jesus.

Mary proclaims the «might» of God because through it «his mercy reaches from age to age». God places his might at the service of compassion. His mercy reaches all generations. Jesus preaches the same message: God is merciful to all. So he says to his disciples of every age: «*Be merciful as your heavenly Father is merciful*». With the heart of a mother, Mary understands, as no one else does, the tenderness of a God who is a Father and a Mother. From the depths of her experience she leads us to the heart of the message of Jesus: God is compassionate love.

Mary also proclaims the God of the poor, for «*he has brought down rulers from their thrones*», leaving them without power to oppress; on the contrary, «*he has lifted up the lowly*», so that they may regain their dignity. From the rich he reclaims what they have stolen from the poor and sends them away empty; the hungry he fills with good things, so they can enjoy a more dignified life. Jesus too announced the same: «*The last shall be first*». Mary leads us to welcome the Good News of Jesus: God is the God of the poor.

Mary shows us, as no one else has done, how to follow Jesus: we proclaim the God of compassion, work for a more fraternal world, and have faith in the Father of the lowly.

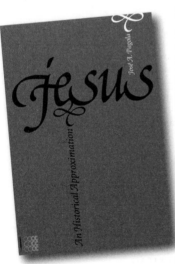

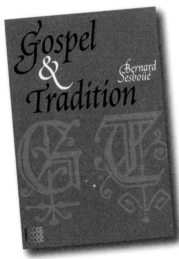

Following in the Footsteps of Jesus
Meditations on the Gospels for Year C

This book was printed on *thin opaque smooth white Bible paper*, using the *Minion* and *Type Embellishments One* font families.

This edition was printed in D'VINNI, S.A., in Bogotá, Colombia, during the last weeks of the ninth month of year two thousand twelve.

Ad publicam lucem datus mense septembre in nativitate Sancte Marie